APOSTLE,
COWBOY STYLE

APOSTLE,
COWBOY STYLE
THE EMERGENCE OF COWBOY MINISTRY

GLENN SMITH

CREATION
HOUSE

Apostle, Cowboy Style by Glenn Smith
Published by Creation House
A Charisma Media Company
600 Rinehart Road
Lake Mary, Florida 32746
www.charismamedia.com

Unless otherwise noted, all Scripture quotations are from the King James Version of the Bible.

Design Director: Justin Evans
Cover design by Terry Clifton

Visit the author's website:
www.rodeocowboyministries.org

Library of Congress CataloginginPublication Data: 2014941151
International Standard Book Number: 978-1-62136-764-2
E-book International Standard Book Number:
978-1-62136-765-9

While the author has made every effort to provide accurate telephone numbers and Internet addresses at the time of publication, neither the publisher nor the author assumes any responsibility for errors or for changes that occur after publication.

14 15 16 17 18 — 987654321
Printed in Canada

DEDICATION

THIS BOOK IS dedicated to cowboys and girls everywhere and, in particular, to the friends and partners of this ministry who have prayed and given so sacrificially to send the news of God's love through His Son, Jesus Christ, to the western world.

Ann and I only regret that because of lack of space many names and incidents equally as exciting as the ones contained in this book have of necessity been deleted in the editing process.

Above all, it is our prayer and heart's desire that this book be used to glorify no one other than He who made it all possible—Jesus, Lord alone.

CONTENTS

FOREWORD

WHEN I READ *Apostle, Cowboy Style*, it stirred me like an old fire horse hearing a bell. My insides jumped and ran; and once again in my heart and mind, I was out there on nothing but my faith as I read about Glenn Smith's experiences with a miracle-working God.

As I read I laughed; I cried. But most of all, I prayed and thanked the Lord Jesus over and over again for allowing me to have a part in this powerful outpouring of the Holy Spirit in the western world.

Glenn and Ann are very special to Gloria and me. They will be to you too by the time you finish reading *Apostle, Cowboy Style*.

Read every word!

Kenneth Copeland

Chapter One
THE COMMISSION

AWAKENED FROM A sound sleep, I sat straight up in bed. It was the latter part of March 1973, around 2:30 A.M. Strangely still, not the tiniest breeze blew—except right around me. Sitting there in bed, I saw bull riders who were "hung up." Their hands were hung in the rope, what we in rodeo circles know as a suicide wrap. I saw the clowns and other bull riders try, to no avail, to get the cowboys loose from the bulls. I saw bronc riders with their feet hung in the stirrups. But the most real and terrifying thing about the vision was: I could see flames flickering behind these cowboys.

I was having, I thought, the most vivid dream in the world. I now know that it was a vision from God. Though I had gotten saved the year before and rejoiced at my newfound love for Jesus, I didn't know anything about visions at that time.

I finally fell into a troubled sleep, puzzling over what exactly the dream meant.

Rodeo is a dangerous sport and a dangerous occupation. I remember, when I was a clown, standing and watching the ambulance drivers carry out on stretchers cowboys who had been gored by bulls, stomped on, or trampled. Once, at a rodeo in Texas, I was getting ready to ride a bull; I was the first bull rider out. The last saddle bronc rider out got bucked out over the horse's head and got his foot hung in the stirrup. It was an awful and sickening sight to see the bronc kick that young man in the head and see the very life flow out of him.

The dream ran over and over through my mind all the following day. I couldn't seem to get away from it. Suddenly it dawned on me: God was trying to tell me something! Those flames I had seen represented hell. Those cowboys He was showing me were dying. They did not know Jesus Christ and were headed to a fiery hell.

I realized then that it was God's way of telling me that He had a call on my life to go and minister to some of the finest professional athletes in the world: the professional rodeo cowboys. (I was later to learn that God's call included cowboys of every kind and the western world in general.)

I went out behind our garage that same day and accepted God's call. I prayed dubiously, "Lord, if I am to minister to those rodeo cowboys, I have no idea how we are going to do this. Lord, You know that up to this point they have been a gospel-hardened bunch. To the best of my knowledge, there has never been a preacher who has gone to them. But, Lord, I am willing." God gave me a peace that He would take care of it and go before me.

I began to search the Scriptures more and more each day. I didn't forget the call God had put on me, but I didn't know how to go about it. I didn't know where to start. I didn't have any idea what to do. I only knew that the concern of my heart was to go to those cowboys and somehow to relate to them the person and love of the Lord Jesus Christ.

I read the Bible diligently and prayed, sometimes all day. I felt that I needed scriptural confirmation of the vision I had seen. I needed scripture that verified my call from God. Somehow, even in my ignorance at that time in my new walk with the Lord, I knew I needed to seek scripture that verified my call from God. It wasn't until later that I learned how important it is to have everything confirmed by the written Word. It is the final authority.

I picked up my Bible. Before I opened it I prayed, "God, I believe that somewhere in the Bible You can speak to me and give me clear direction as to where You want me to go, exactly what You want me to do, and how You want me to do it. Lord, if You will just show me out of Your Word, I will be more than happy to take off and do whatever it is." I opened my Bible. The second chapter of the Book of Ezekiel leaped out at me. This is what it says: "Son of man, I send thee to the children of Israel, to a rebellious nation that hath rebelled against me: they and their fathers have transgressed against me, even unto this very day" (v. 3).

As I read that, the words seemed at least two feet high in my mind and heart. I knew God was speaking to me. I read on, deeply convicted.

> For they are impudent children and stiff hearted. I do send thee unto them; and thou shalt say unto them, Thus saith the Lord God.

> And they, whether they will hear, or whether
> they will forbear, (for they are a rebellious
> house,) yet shall know that there hath been a
> prophet among them.
>
> —EZEKIEL 2:4–5

That settled it. God had indeed called me into the ministry. He now confirmed by His written Word what He had put in my heart.

I wasn't ignorant concerning the task; I knew it would not be simple. I had begun to rodeo in 1950 at age fifteen. Rodeo remained at the center of my life for many years after that. I received my Professional Rodeo Cowboys Association (PRCA) card in 1955 and unenthusiastically became of age to receive my gold card in 1986.

Many people don't understand the ways of rodeo cowboys. Their travel time is very precious to them, and when they are in the arena competing they don't want to talk to anyone, not even their wife or best buddy. Their mind is fixed on competing, winning.

In the years I was competing, it was understood that if you didn't drink, cuss, chase women, and fight, you were not accepted. I figured this was still the attitude, in general, and in 1973 I was right. It has changed drastically since then.

As I began to pray and seek God for more direction, once again in the early hours of the morning, He showed me the same vision. Flames danced behind competing cowboys in distress. This time I knew I had to share with my wife, Ann. I had been reluctant to do so because, long before, when I quit my last job as a rodeo clown, I had promised her I would never go back. But this was God.

Ann was out of town at the time visiting friends in Virginia. I decided to break the news to her by phone. I told her God had been dealing with me and had revealed to me that He had a call on my life and a special assignment for me. To my utter surprise, she said, "Honey, I know that, and I have known it for over six months. One night when you were asleep and I was restless I went into the living room to pray. I was seeking God's direction for our lives. The Lord told me that in His eyes you were a missionary evangelist, or apostolic evangelist, that you were to go preach the gospel. But He told me to be quiet until you told me."

Startled, I reluctantly asked her, "Did He tell you where I was to go?"

Ann answered, "Yes. He said you were to go and minister to the professional rodeo cowboys and the western world."

Relieved beyond description, I began to praise the Lord. I was excited over how thorough He was in this thing. What peace came over me!

THE TRANSITION

My hunger for the Word of God continued. I began to devour it. I started seeing things in the Bible that I had never heard any preacher preach. I began to see that God said He could and would supply every need my family and I had. Philippians 4:19 became alive to me: "But my

God shall supply all your need according to his riches in glory by Christ Jesus." I kept asking, "Lord, what does this mean to me?"

I continuously sought God for clear direction on how to proceed. I questioned, "How are You going to take care of my family if I abandon my business and go on the road? How am I to manage all the travel expenses?"

Ann and I began to listen to cassette tapes. Preaching and teaching cassettes had just become popular in the early seventies. I knew there was something I needed to see or hear, but I didn't know what.

One day I went to the mailbox and there was a package from Fort Worth, Texas, addressed to "Glenn Smith." In it were six tapes by Brother Kenneth Copeland. Kenneth is now a dear friend of mine, but at the time, I had no idea who he was.

These tapes were Brother Kenneth's teaching on receiving the promises of God—receiving God's supply and abundance according to His Word.

I sat down that day and got my Bible. I listened to those tapes, and God began to show me things that excited my heart. He was speaking to me through a man I had never heard of, never met. Yet everything I had cried out for God to show me, Brother Kenneth was talking about on those tapes.

I sat for hours listening to this man from Fort Worth preach. I would stop the tape recorder and read it out of my Bible. I was so elated with what God was speaking to me through those tapes that my insides were literally jumping. I called Ann in and began to share with her these things, and God began to reveal them to her. We could see that God, in His supernatural love and wisdom, was somehow going to take care of us!

I was in a successful contracting business at the time. I had painters, paper hangers, and others working for me. Although I would go on the job each day, my interest was no longer there. My mind would turn to the Word and what God had told me to do. One day I cried out to Jesus, "Lord, what do I do from here? I know that I am called. I believe that You can provide our finances and open doors for me. But, Lord, what do I do?"

Suddenly, I decided to go to my pickup and listen to the only Christian radio station I could get. Just as I switched the radio on I heard the preacher say, "Do you want to know what God's perfect will is in your life? Read the Book of James!"

Right then I got my Bible and began to read the Book of James. I never got to chapter two. As I read James 1, verse 22, it worked me over: "But be ye doers of the word, and not hearers only, deceiving your own selves." I knew it was time for me to start doing what little I knew about God's will for my life.

One night shortly thereafter I was awakened from sleep. I heard a voice, deep inside of me. I knew it was the Lord. He said, "Give up your business tomorrow. Your job for Me begins now."

I said, "Yes, Lord."

The next morning I called my hands in. I had enough money in the bank to pay off all my workers and give them an extra two weeks' salary. I got on the phone and found every one of them a job with other contractors there in Austin. In less than an hour I found myself out of business and in the ministry.

I committed myself to prayer and reading God's Word as never before. I sought God's face more diligently than ever. I listened to those tapes of Brother Copeland's over and over again.

I began to do what I call some "sanctified" reasoning. God had shown me that the only effective way to reach the cowboys was to make myself available twenty-four hours a day to be a witness to them and of spiritual help in any and every way they would permit. That could not be done by running to a rodeo for a day, returning home, and then traveling to another rodeo halfway across the United States. I would need to follow the cowboys from rodeo to rodeo. I had to have living accommodations. I knew I could not take our only good car and travel on the rodeo circuit. To be able to minister effectively, I would have to have at least a pickup and camper.

Now that our contracting business had been closed down, Ann and I were daily trusting God that according to His Word, He was not only giving us direction but also supplying our every need. And God was doing exactly that.

Money came in supernaturally to pay our house rent, other bills, and provide groceries. No one in our family lacked for anything. Our daughters, Pam and Kay, were learning to trust the Lord for their needs too. Kay, then about twelve, got busy believing the Lord for seventy-five dollars for some clothes. She thanked God daily and fervently. One day the phone rang and a man asked for Kay. Her little face shone with delight during that conversation. When she hung up, she told us that a man in our local church had been praying, and the Lord instructed him to call Kay and tell her he had a check for her to buy new clothes. The check exceeded her seventy-five dollar request. Needless to say, we rejoiced with her.

I had people call me and tell me that they had beaten me out of money on a business deal as far back as a year before. For some reason it strangely bothered them now, and they wanted to pay me and make it right. A man called Ann one day from another city quite a few miles away. We hardly knew him. He felt he was to send us one hundred dollars and wanted our address. That was the exact amount we had to have immediately to pay our phone bill. Ann would pray, the girls and I would agree, and God would send people with whom we were not even acquainted to give us money. God was proving to us that we could rely on Him to truly supply our every need as were obedient to Him. It was an exciting time in our lives.

At the beginning of this, our family's faith walk, Ann had gotten before God and asked Him for a scripture for us to stand upon. She and the girls were going to be alone while I traveled—in the early days of the ministry—and she wanted a promise from God, something she could count on. He gave her 1 Kings 17:14: "For thus saith the Lord God of Israel, The barrel of meal shall not waste, neither shall the cruse of oil fail, until the day that the Lord sendeth rain upon the earth." He has faithfully performed it, even unto today.

Pam, Kay, and Ann had placed themselves in agreement with me upon the Word of God that I had my badly needed pickup and camper. Matthew 18:19 promises, "Again I say unto you, That if two of you shall agree on earth as touching any thing that they shall ask, it shall be done for them of my Father which is in heaven." Several friends from our local church, including our pastor and his wife, Brother Kenneth and Betty Morgan, were standing in agreement with us. We had received, by faith, my pickup and camper, and I had been thanking God almost constantly for the manifestation of it.

One night while we were driving to our local church service, my attention was suddenly drawn to a car lot on my left. As I turned in there Ann asked, "What are you doing?"

"I don't know. The Lord just told me to pull in here," I answered. Right in front of me, as I stopped the car, was a Ford pickup. Ann and I walked over to it. I told her, "I believe God is telling me this is my truck."

"It is pretty," she commented. "And if it is God, then we need to pray over it and ask Him to bring it into the ministry." We laid hands on the pickup, and I prayed and received the truck as mine into the ministry to go forth and spread the gospel of the Lord Jesus Christ.

Just as I said, "Amen," I heard the shuffling of feet behind me. It was the car salesman, and he had heard us praying. He looked at me, as only an unbeliever can, and said, "Sir, I am sorry. This pickup is sold. A man came just a couple of hours ago and put a cash deposit on it."

I looked at the man and boldly declared, "That deal will not go through because the truck is mine."

The salesman replied apologetically, "I don't know about that. All I know is that I have money on the deal, and it looks perfect." I assured the fellow in the name of Jesus the truck was mine.

On the way home from church that night we again passed by the lot where the truck sat. Ann and I briefly thanked God that the truck was ours and believed we received it according to Mark 11:24: "Therefore I say unto you, What things soever ye desire, when ye pray, believe that ye receive them, and ye shall have them." We had already fulfilled Mark 11:23: "For verily I say unto you, That whosoever shall say unto this mountain, Be thou removed, and be thou cast into the sea; and shall not doubt in his heart, but shall believe that those things which he saith shall come to pass; he shall have whatsoever he saith." We had spoken to the pickup and called it into the ministry.

The next day around noon the salesman called and said, "I don't know why, but my deal on the truck fell through. If you still want it, come on down, make a cash deposit on it, and we will get the papers handled for you." The Lord had promised me that He had called me and would supply my every need. He did just that. He worked out a supernatural deal, and in three days I drove the pickup off the lot. I knew then that God's Word worked. I didn't know how He had done it; I just knew He had.

Next was the camper. Ann, the girls, and I had prayed

and received a very nice camper to go on the back of the truck. We believed God to show us where the camper was.

One afternoon some friends had come over to take us out to eat, and we were driving around. We passed a camper dealer, and I said, "Stop a minute, and let's look at those campers." Immediately I spied a pretty little camper and knew it was the one I wanted to put on my new pickup. It was just exactly what I needed. Our friends agreed with us in prayer. I began to praise and thank God for it, just as I had the pickup.

Until this point the Lord had not shown me the site of my first missionary trip. It was the third week of May in 1973 when I was again awakened out of my sleep. The words, "Cassville, Missouri," kept rotating in my mind. I had never heard of the town; I didn't even know there was such a place. I got up and looked at the map. Sure enough, there was a town called Cassville, Missouri! I next found my latest publication of the *Rodeo Sports News*, and wouldn't you know it: in Cassville, Missouri, there was to be a professional rodeo. God said to me, "Go." Next came the words, "Greenville, Texas." I went back to the *Sports News*, and there was the Greenville, Texas, rodeo. It was the weekend before Cassville. I got out my map and charted my route—first to Greenville, next to Cassville.

I thanked God for showing me where to launch my missionary venture. I was to leave on a Wednesday. The camper I was to live in had not appeared by sight, although I knew in my spirit it was mine. I kept praising God and reminding Him that He had called me into this ministry.

I knew He was not going to send me out ill-equipped. I must have prayed and praised fifty times a day.

Tuesday came; no camper. Ann and I proceeded as if it were already sitting on the pickup. We packed my clothes and took care of details.

All I knew about the faith walk was what I had heard on Kenneth Copeland's tapes, but I knew that if it worked for him, it would work for me. I had read in God's Word that He was no respecter of persons. I loaded my truck on Wednesday and walked back to the house. I leaned down to kiss Ann and our girls good-bye. I was off to tell a lost world about the love of Jesus, with still no camper visible.

As I was about to walk out the door, the phone rang. Passing by, I picked it up. The man on the other end of the line asked, "Is this Glenn Smith?"

"Yes."

The fellow identified himself as the manager of a certain camper sales company. He said, "Mr. Smith, I have been instructed to tell you that the Lord has a camper here for your pickup. If you will come right down here, we will put it on your truck and get you on the road."

I just started screaming in his ear, "Hallelujah! Thank You, Jesus!" I was laughing, crying, and praising God— all at the same time. The man on the phone patiently listened to me.

Finally the Lord got through to me and said, "Why don't you ask him where he is?" I got his address and drove there. It was the identical camper that we had prayed and received weeks before. It was put in place on my truck—a beautiful picture of God's faithfulness.

Chapter Two
INTO THE WILDERNESS

JOURNEYED TOWARD GREENVILLE with very few dollars in my pocket. At the time I left home, Ann and I had maybe seventy or eighty dollars between us. Though we had been learning to trust the Lord for our finances the past few months, we seldom had an excess. The last ninety days we had been giving financially out of our need. We would pray and ask God where He wanted us to give, even above our tithes. Even though it appeared that we were living hand to mouth, God was teaching us, at this early stage of our ministry, vital scriptural principles for our survival.

Jesus taught clearly the seed principle in Mark, chapter 4. Ann and I saw from our early Christian days that in order to reap, we must sow. And it stood to reason that the more we would sow, the more we would reap.

With some gas money and very little for food, I stopped at a service station between Dallas and Greenville. In 1973 there was a big gasoline scare. People were frantic about it. In those days gas was being rationed. It was hard to get, and there were long lines at service stations.

Stepping out of my truck, I noticed a well-dressed man putting gas in his car. He was right next to me. I felt the urge to tell him about Jesus. I waited until he had put the gas in his car, and I said, "Sir, do you know Jesus Christ as your Lord and Savior?" I will never forget the look on his face. He looked at me as if I were some kind of nut. He proceeded to tell me he was the pastor of a big church in some town—I missed the name. He didn't get around to telling me if he knew Jesus. So I asked him again.

He answered me, "I am the pastor of one of the largest churches in Philadelphia. How dare you ask me if I know Jesus Christ."

When I went to pay the attendant for my gas, a young man was standing there, and I asked him, "Hey, brother, do you know the Lord Jesus Christ?"

He replied, "Yes, I do." We began to share about the Lord.

"I just tried to witness to that man out there in the blue Buick," I told him.

"Well, praise God, that's my pastor. I'm not really sure if he is even saved."

I saw right then how important it is to obey the Spirit of the Lord when He impresses us to witness and how necessary it is to take no man's salvation for granted.

I drove on to Greenville, found the rodeo grounds, and parked in the contestant area. I began to intercede for the cowboys and girls.

The next morning I went to the Holiday Inn for coffee. The waitress had just brought me a cup when a well-dressed and equally well-mannered cowboy sat down beside me. He introduced himself, saying, "Hello, my name is Hadley Barrett."

"I'm Glenn Smith."

"Glenn, what do you do?"

He almost spilled his coffee when I told him I was an evangelist, sent by God to share Jesus with rodeo cowboys. "Boy! You have your work cut out for you," he exclaimed.

I assured him, "That's all right. God can handle anything, Hadley."

Later that day I saw Hadley talking to a group of cowboys.

As I walked by he said, "Well, here he is right now. Come here, Glenn, and let me introduce you to some of these people." Thus, God began to make contacts to open the doors to the rodeo ministry.

It was best that I didn't know what a tough year I had ahead of me. There had never been anyone full-time on the circuit carrying the gospel of Jesus Christ. Even though I wore Wranglers and boots and looked just as cowboy as they did, from day one I was marked as "the preacher."

My time at Greenville didn't abound with witnessing opportunities, other than Hadley. I spent most of my days in my camper reading the Word and praying. At night, I would circulate among the cowboys and try to meet as many of them as I could. When they found out what I was doing there, they would suddenly remember they needed to go check on something. They used all sorts of excuses to get away from me so I wouldn't preach to them.

I resisted the desire to feel sorry for myself. After all, I only wanted to tell these guys there is a better way of life. I began to feel condemned—like I was doing something wrong that was preventing them from listening to me. Yet I didn't know anything else to do or not to do. I resorted to spending more time in prayer.

I left Greenville and headed to Cassville, Missouri. On the way I prayed and asked God to do something to prove Himself to me and to show me how the ministry was to go.

After parking on the rodeo grounds, the first person I ran into was Hadley Barrett, the rodeo announcer. "I'm going over to put up my PA system," he said, "Would you like to go with me?" I went, and we talked about the Lord. I didn't push him.

Later in the day, Hadley told me the rodeo committee wanted to open the rodeo with a prayer. He asked if I would be willing to give the invocation for them. I was glad to honor his request.

I didn't preach a sermon, exactly, in that prayer, but I did get in a plug for Jesus. I asked God's protection over the contestants and the pickup men. One of the pickup men later commented that I was the only preacher he had ever heard who prayed especially for them. That blessed me. I knew already that the cowboys were listening.

It was in Cassville that I met a top-notch rodeo clown and beautiful Christian man from California, Wilbur Plaugher. Wilbur, his wife, Ruth, and I got together and shared about Jesus. I was absolutely thrilled to find another Christian on the circuit!

God had been dealing with Wilbur to witness and be more open to the cowboys. He and six other men met at a rodeo in Phoenix, Arizona, in 1974 and started the cowboy chapter of the Fellowship of Christian Athletes.

Loneliness would overwhelm me at times. I would go to my camper and just cry, "God, if You sent me here, why don't any of these guys want to listen to me when I mention Jesus?"

During the Cassville rodeo, Jiggs Beutler, the rodeo producer, asked me if I knew anything about working the rodeo. When I told him I followed the rodeo circuit for years, he asked me to help him. I said I would. Working in the arena, running scores, I became acquainted with a lot of the cowboys.

At coffee in the mornings the cowboys would come and talk to me until it got around that I was a minister. Then they would suddenly find it necessary to talk to someone at another table, take their coffee, and leave. I kept praying, because I knew I was where God had sent me.

The Cassville rodeo ended, and Jiggs brought me a check for working the labor list. It was maybe forty dollars, enough to buy gas, eat something, and start back home. God multiplied my gas all the way home. Every time I stopped to get the two-dollar limit, it seemed to go farther.

Home again, I shared with Ann my disappointment. I had not been able to witness to the cowboys in the way I had anticipated. She encouraged me as we again discussed my call. We knew that God had sent me and that I had to go again.

Very few people at this point knew that I was called to the ministry. My church felt led to support our ministry with ninety dollars each week. That took some pressure off of me. (After a period of several months, God launched us into a totally nondenominational ministry and instructed us to discontinue the acceptance of the weekly support.)

In prayer, the latter part of June, I felt strongly impressed to go to Springdale, Arkansas, to the big rodeo that was held every Fourth of July. I said, "Lord, if this is You, I know you will provide the money to go."

When it came time for me to leave Ann and I had the sum of forty dollars to our name. I knew that wouldn't even buy enough gas to get me to Springdale, Arkansas. And what was my family to use for food while I was gone? I really questioned God. I prayed, "God, if this is really You, then show me what to do." It flashed through my mind, "Take thirty-five dollars." I thought, "Man, if I take that it will only leave five dollars for Ann and the girls. I'm going to be gone at least ten days." I muttered, "Lord, if this is truly You, confirm it through Ann. And show her about the money, please."

The next morning Ann came to the breakfast table and said, "I don't know if this is just me or the Lord, but I feel you are to go to Springdale and take thirty-five of that forty dollars with you." I couldn't doubt that this was God. He was saying, "You go, and I will provide. You be obedient, and I will take care of you."

Ann put some sandwiches, canned soup, instant milk, and coffee in my camper, and off I drove toward Springdale. I knew that from a natural standpoint, I would never make it. It gave me a perfect opportunity to pray hour upon hour and trust God. I continued to seek Him about how this faith walk Brother Copeland talked about would work consistently in our lives and ministry. God's Word says He is a rewarder of those who diligently seek Him, and I was diligently seeking Him with all my heart.

I had two dollars left when I came to a little town in Arkansas. It was getting dark, and my gasoline gauge was almost on empty. There were no stations open. I kept driving, knowing that God would somehow intervene. I had just topped a mountain when I heard the pickup spit, cough, and die. I was right by a roadside park.

There were no cars coming by at that time of night. People were not on the road unless they had to be because of the extremely limited gasoline. I got out two sandwiches that I had been saving all day. I sat at the picnic table watching the squirrels run around. I could see God everywhere. It was almost dark, and it was a beautiful spot. In the stillness I cried out to God, "Lord, what is going on? I just don't understand. I am trying to do what You want me to do, and I have two dollars left. I don't have any gas, and there is no one coming by. What am I going to do?"

Words, as though they were a neon sign, appeared in my mind: "The fervent prayer of a righteous man availeth much." I kept seeing those words over and over. I knew they were from the Book of James, but I didn't even know what they meant. I said, "Lord, I'm just a cowboy, and I don't understand what You are saying. If I knew what a fervent prayer was, I would pray it right now! Oh, Lord, please intervene. I ask You in the name of Your Son, Jesus."

I began to see in my mind, as you would on television, Jesus standing and ministering to hundreds of people. They were hungry. I saw a small boy come by with some fish and loaves of bread. I saw Jesus take that little bit of nothing and lift it up to God to bless it. In my spirit I saw Jesus feed thousands of people.

The Lord then spoke, "Go put your finger in the gas tank and praise and thank Me for multiplying it, and I will do it." I thought, "This is surely not God! I must be hallucinating. Those sandwiches must have been bad. God wouldn't tell me to do that!"

Yet, I had an inner compulsion to do what God said. By that time it really was dark. Still, I looked both ways. It would be embarrassing for someone to see me with my finger in the gas tank, head bowed, and eyes closed. No one was coming, so I stuck my finger in the gas tank. I said, "God, Jesus multiplied the loaves and fish. I believe You are a God that can do anything. I even believe You could raise up a gas refinery here on this hill tonight." I put the cap back on and got in the truck with my heart full of faith and my head full of doubt.

I turned the key, and the pickup started. I slipped it into gear, went down the mountain, and up another, on and on. I praised God in every way that I knew, with every breath.

About thirty miles later, I spied a *Y* in the road with a small service station. I headed for it. As I pulled in, I reached down to turn the key off. Before I could do so, the truck stopped running. I was so high in the Spirit it was hard to come down. I looked down at the mileage again; I had driven thirty-eight miles on the power, goodness, and mercy of God!

The station appeared to be closing. The lights were being turned out. I ran in and said, "Oh, ma'am, I need some gasoline. I am so glad I got here before you closed."

The woman replied, "Well, maybe I can help you; no one can help me." I asked what she meant, and she poured out her heart to me. She had planned to close the station and commit suicide that very night. She said her life was a mess, and she couldn't see a way out.

I thought, "Isn't God something? He takes this cowboy who is so high on His miracle-working power and grace and hooks me up with this lady who is in the depths of despair." I began to share the love of Jesus with her. I told her what Jesus could do, how great He was, and what He had just done for me. She began to cry. I asked, "Wouldn't you like to take Jesus into your heart?" She said she would. I took her by the hand and led her in the sinner's prayer. Then she really broke down and cried. I cried with her.

Suddenly we both began to laugh, and she questioned, "What was it you wanted when you came in here?" I reminded her of the gasoline I needed. That lady gave me a whole tank of gasoline!

I left, shouting and rejoicing that God was God. I still had my two dollars. I drove on up the road and stopped at a nice roadside park. I saw a sign that said,

Overnight hook-ups: two dollars. No one was there to take my money, so I found a place to park and went over and took a hot shower. The next morning I made some coffee and went to the office to pay the bill. I noticed he had a sign on the wall that said, For God so loved the world. That was all that it said. That was enough. When his wife came to help me, we shared the Lord.

I told her what I was doing and what God had been doing in my life. She wouldn't take my money. She invited me, anytime I was in the area, to stop in "on the house." She and her husband considered it a privilege to help anyone who was going out to communicate the love and saving power of the Lord Jesus.

My excitement had mounted when I left the camping area. God was so real to me, proving again and again His call on my life and His provisions for it. No matter how impossible the situation looked, He was the almighty God. I could hear Him saying over and over, "I AM THAT I AM." What a reassurance that was.

I drove to DeQueen, Arkansas. I missed the turn I needed to take to Springdale. As I was trying to get back to the right highway, I drove past a huge Baptist church. I had just noticed the sign when my pickup stopped running. I knew I wasn't out of gas. I decided to go into the church and get a drink of water. The first man I saw was the youth pastor. He kindly gave me the water as I told him what I was doing.

"Do you know an evangelist by the name of Manley Beasley?" he asked me. I knew him well. God had used Brother Manley mightily in our lives when we were baby

Christians. He meant a lot to me. This pastor had gone to one of Manley's meetings and had been so blessed. His church was starting a tape library for shut-ins, and he wanted some of Brother Manley's tapes. He asked me if I had any with me. I told him, "You know, I do. I have eight of them." I found them—and two more tapes I thought might be of interest to him—and waited while he copied them.

As I left, the youth pastor said, "Here, take this twenty dollars in the name of Jesus. I am glad to be a part of your ministry to the cowboys."

I praised God. I now had twenty-two dollars and a tank of gas. I was beginning to see the harvest of my financial sowing.

I walked back to the pickup and laid my hands on it. I said, "Truck, in the name of Jesus, I command you to take me to Springdale, Arkansas." I hopped into it, turned the key, and the engine started. I took off again, praising the Lord.

Reaching Springdale in the afternoon, I found a place to hook up where the cowboys parked. I climbed into the camper and began to praise the Lord for all He had done for me.

Later that day, I walked over to the arena. The first person I ran into was Hadley Barrett. He told me that Jiggs was looking for someone to run scores and work the calf chute. While I was thinking about it, I heard my mouth say, "I'll do it." Jiggs came by later and said he appreciated the help and told me what the job paid. It was interesting to watch God place me with men who, although unaware of it, were being used to promote the moving of the Holy Spirit on the rodeo circuit.

Late one afternoon, as we were preparing for the rodeo, I saw a vivid demonstration of the enemy at work trying to stop the preaching of the gospel to cowboys and girls. I was sitting on the fender of a horse trailer talking about the Lord to Hadley. A certain cowboy came riding up on a horse that weighed about twelve hundred pounds and stood about sixteen hands high. He heard me talking. He didn't know he was being used by the devil.

I saw him take down his rope and tie-on hard and fast. In other words, the rope was tied to the saddle horn. The cowboy rode up to me, slipped the loop over my foot, jerked the slack out of it, and proceeded to ride away with me on the other end of the rope. I heard him say, "What is your God going to do for you now?"

I could see I was in trouble. I knew that the man was capable of dragging me out in the parking lot through pickups and trucks. There were many cowboys standing around watching the incident that evening.

For a few steps, Hadley ran beside me and held me up so I could stay on my feet. There was no way I could get my foot out of the rope. I answered the cowboy's question. "I don't know what my God is going to do, but I know that He loves you, and if you drag me to death, the last thing I am going to say is, '(I called him by name), Jesus loves you.'" When I said that, I guess it embarrassed him, and he stopped.

He said, "Take that rope off your foot." I did, and he whirled and rode away.

From that point on, I began to cry out to God for that man's salvation. Every time he would come around he would persecute me, saying nasty things about me and about the Lord. Jesus reminded me, "Blessed are they who are persecuted for My sake."

I did not realize at the time how many cowboys were listening and watching what was going on. They began to see God's love through me. It certainly was nothing I did, because it was all I could do to keep from throwing the Bible away and walking out on God. Yet, God had begun to intervene supernaturally, casting His net of love and salvation over the rodeo circuit. It didn't matter that I could not yet see exactly how and what He was doing. He was working in the recesses of hearts.

The Springdale rodeo finally over, I took off for home. I was driving down the road when it dawned on me I had gotten off on the wrong highway. Now, I am a very precise fellow where directions are concerned. Yet, I had missed my highway.

Driving considerably faster down the same highway was one of the clowns who had worked Springdale, Dan Willis, one of the top bullfighters. His wife, Jan, was driving, and Dan was sitting in the passenger seat in the front. As they went past, I saw him turn around and look at me.

Thirty miles later, as I rounded a curve in the road, Dan Willis was in the middle of the highway, flagging me down. I pulled over, and he got in the truck. "Where is Jan?" I asked. She had gone on into town, he told me. Puzzled, I questioned, "What are you doing out here?"

Dan came right to the point: "I needed to talk to you about the Lord."

How thrilled I was! I had been trying for over a month to talk to cowboys, and no one, except Hadley, would listen to me. Now someone had actually waved me down to talk to me about Jesus. I had a real, live cowboy in my pickup who wanted to hear about Jesus, and no one else was there.

As Dan and I continued down the road, he began to tell me how God was dealing in his life. He had heard that I was a preacher and had been wanting to talk to me, but for some reason he had missed me at the rodeo. His wife, Jan, was a Christian and had been praying for him. The Holy Spirit brought him under conviction. I plainly shared with Dan God's plan of salvation. (The Word of God took root, for I was soon to hear that Dan had given his heart to Jesus.)

We arrived at the restaurant where Jan was waiting, and Dan bought my meal. I rejoiced, because I wanted to take some money home to show Ann how God had provided just as He said He would!

Home once more, Ann and I praised the Lord for all He had done. While I was gone, one man felt impressed to send one hundred dollars. Another stopped by the house and brought money.

We could see without a doubt that God wanted the gospel preached on the rodeo circuit, that His Word was true, and that if we would abide in it, He would surely supply all our need.

Chapter Three
DEEPER INTO THE WILDERNESS

THE BIG CHEYENNE Frontier Days rodeo was coming up in July. I began to trust the Lord for the money to go. I knew that over one thousand cowboys would be there competing. I was certain that was the rodeo where God was going to break my ministry loose.

While I was still seeking God about Cheyenne, a young cowboy, no longer active on the circuit, was introduced to me. His name was Phil Underwood. Phil expressed his concern for the lost cowboys and cowgirls and came frequently to our house. We shared the desire to reach the western world with the love of Jesus.

A few days before Cheyenne began, Phil called and said, "My pickup is broken down. I was going to Cheyenne on my vacation. Now I feel God would have me go with you in your pickup and help pay your expenses. I could help you do some witnessing and still take in the rodeo." That was my answer to prayer. God had moved on Phil to finance the trip.

Taking our bedrolls and a few staples, we took off to Cheyenne, Wyoming, to win the world for Jesus. However, it didn't exactly turn out that way. Phil and I spent five days trying to pass out tracts, and few would take them. We tried to witness about Jesus, and no one would listen.

When we had been there several nights, the master cylinder on the pickup went out. We didn't have enough money to get it fixed. One night while Phil and I were talking about the situation, the experience of the empty gas tank suddenly came to mind. I told Phil, "Tomorrow, we will lay hands on that cylinder in the name of the Lord Jesus Christ. The Bible says that whatever we ask believing, that He will do. We will agree, and I believe God will supernaturally fix it." Phil agreed.

The next morning we raised the hood on the truck and placed our hands on the master cylinder. We began to pray, asking God to fix that thing. I got in it, put it in low gear, and took off. The brakes on that truck worked better than they ever had before. It was a tremendous encouragement to our faith.

Our main purpose for being in Cheyenne, however, seemed to remain unfulfilled. Neither of us led anyone to Jesus. We did meet a young pastor and spoke in his church.

As we left for home I began to think, "This is not right. I have certainly missed the calling of God here. There is something that I should be doing that I am not doing. I can't understand. If God is calling me to this ministry, why am I not seeing any fruit?" The doubts began to come hard and fast.

I traveled to other rodeos close to home. I went to the Oklahoma State Fair and again worked on the labor list—Jiggs Beutler was the contractor. I ran scores and saddled the pickup horses.

In spite of my apparent fruitlessness, God was miraculously all this time supplying all our needs financially. God supernaturally cared for Ann and the girls while I was gone on my missionary trips. Actually, they weren't missionary trips in my sight. I began to think they were a waste of time.

September, October, and November were gone. I had seen no cowboys come to Jesus. I continued to pass out tracts, to no apparent avail. Most of the day, I prayed for the cowboys, and at night I tried to corner someone and talk to him about the Lord. It just didn't work. I was depressed spiritually and mentally. I had no idea then that it was Satan trying to stop me from reaching those cowboys.

The first year I went to the National Finals Rodeo in Oklahoma City, I took Brother Copeland's tapes that had come earlier that year. I listened to them and prayed all day and went to the performances at night. I tried to witness, but the Finals seemed no place to witness. I placed tracts in strategic places. When I checked later they would be all over the floor and in the trash. I thought, "God, everybody is against me out here. Are You really in on this thing?" Yet, deep in my spirit I knew He was. I knew that I must be missing it somewhere.

My money was running very low, and I was operating from day to day, meal to meal. Right before the end of the Finals, I ran completely out of money. I didn't have a dime left. I had nothing to eat. I didn't have money to buy gasoline to get home.

I decided to go to the camper and listen to the Copeland tapes. I put a tape on and got comfortable. Brother Kenneth was talking about a time in his early ministry when he had come to a place of great financial need. He had to have some money. He read in the Word where it says, "But lay up for yourselves treasures in heaven, where neither moth nor rust doth corrupt, and where thieves do not break through nor steal" (Matt. 6:20). He went before God and asked Him to dip down in that treasure chest that he had been laying up in heaven and give him one hundred dollars.

I thought about all the times I had given love offerings to missionaries. It was very cold that December day in Oklahoma City when I got down on my knees in the camper and prayed, "Oh, God, I have laid up treasures in heaven, and I need to make a withdrawal right now. I need one hundred dollars out of my treasure chest, and Lord, I sure would like to have it today."

I had barely finished praying when a man I didn't know knocked on my door inquiring about another cowboy. As we talked, the man asked who I was, and what I did. When I told him, he said, "Well, praise the Lord." He was a believer, a brother in Christ. He invited me to his home for an early Christmas dinner. His son was home and had brought with him a Jewish friend who was very interested in knowing more about the Lord Jesus. He asked that I not only come for dinner but also that I pray about sharing Jesus with this young Jewish boy; I accepted.

During the dinner that day I got a chance to minister about Jesus to the Jewish boy. Tears rolled down his cheeks as I shared with him. He took his linen napkin and wiped his face. He said, "I want to believe that so very much. I am so empty on the inside."

I wanted to twist his arm and say, "Pray now and receive Jesus." But the Lord restrained me. "You have said all I intended you to say," He told me. "Now just be quiet and finish your dinner."

Late that afternoon, I needed to round up my hat and coat and return to the rodeo grounds. When I located them on a bed in a bedroom, I saw something lying in my hat. It was a one hundred dollar bill! I didn't know which member of the family put that money in my hat, but I knew God had heard and answered my prayer.

God repeatedly demonstrated that He was in this ministry. It clearly wasn't He who was preventing people from receiving Jesus. I figured it had to be something I was doing.

I traveled to every rodeo I could reasonably reach during the first three months of the following year, God supernaturally supplying the ways and means for me to get to them. I was beginning to meet more cowboys on the circuit. Instead of running away when they saw me coming, they would stay around. When I witnessed about Jesus, they would listen to me but make no decision. They gave no indication they were really *hearing* what I was saying. Entering my second year of ministry, I became extremely discouraged.

Driving home from the last rodeo, I let thoughts from the enemy enter my mind. I began to feel sorry for myself. In fact, I had a big pity party right there on the highway. I became almost convinced that people who told me I had missed God were right.

Ann and the girls were glad to see me, but I was not fit company. I was down and plain mad at God. I thought He had not fulfilled His part of the bargain. Here I had gone and sacrificed and had not led one cowboy to Jesus Christ.

All I wanted to do was lay down and die. I said these words out loud, "God, I believe I am of sound mind, and I realize what I am going to say to You is going to be judged, but at this point I do not care. Lord, I want You to know right now that I quit. I don't care what You have called me to do. I am not going to do it. I am through. I don't care if every one of those people die and go to hell. I am not going anymore."

My oration upset my wife tremendously. She fell to her knees by the kitchen table and began to intercede for me, "Heavenly Father, please forgive him. Lord, don't hear his prayer. Oh, God, please forgive him. He doesn't know what he is saying." All the time I was thinking, "Yes, I do know what I am saying. I'm just through. I am not going another time. I will never go to another rodeo."

But God, in His mercy and grace, prevented His plan from being thwarted.

For two or three days I deliberately rebelled. I didn't

read my Bible or pray. I resisted thinking about God. I did what I wanted to do.

One morning I discovered a flat on the car. I was down on my knees loosening the lug bolts. I began to think about what I had done. I reasoned, "I'm in a position of prayer. I might ought to tell God I'm sorry for what I've said and done." I looked up. "Father God, I am so sorry. I didn't mean to quit. I don't want to quit. I ask you to forgive me for grieving Your Spirit and for being mad at You, for neglecting You and Your Word for these past few days. I ask You to forgive me in the name of Jesus." A wonderful, warm peace dropped over me. The Spirit of God demonstrated His love for me.

Returning to the house, I picked up my Bible. It fell out of my hand and dropped on the floor. As I reached to pick it up, I saw that it had fallen open to the second chapter of the Book of Ezekiel. Thinking what a coincidence that was, I picked it up, simultaneously hearing the voice of the Lord speak in my heart. "My son, read that again, will you, please?"

I began to read, once more, the scripture which God had used to call me into the ministry. This time, however, I saw something by the divine revelation of the Holy Spirit that I'd never seen before. It was in verse 7: "And thou shalt speak my words unto them, whether they will hear, or whether they will forbear: for they are most rebellious."

By revelation of the Holy Spirit I saw what I had done. I had tried to establish a ministry in myself. I had done everything I knew to do to promote the ministry, and all the time God was saying, "You just go and say, 'Thus saith the Lord God.'" I was quick to repent. "Oh, God, I see it is not me but You." He agreed.

I turned in my Bible to Galatians 2:20: "I am crucified with Christ: nevertheless I live; yet not I, but Christ liveth in me: and the life which I now live in the flesh I live by the faith of the Son of God, who loved me, and gave himself for me." It was so alive in me. I was seeing it for the first time. The ministry was the Lord's, not mine. I merely had to go and make myself available to the cowboys. From that point forward, the Lord's plan began to unfold.

At the very next rodeo I went out of the way to get *me* out of the picture. In fact, I probably got too extreme; I just wanted to know that it was all the Lord. I said, "Lord, this is what I am going to do. I want to serve You, and You know I do. I believe You have called me here, and Lord, to make sure it is totally You, I am going to buy some popcorn and a Coke and crawl up into the top of the grandstand. I'm going to sit there and watch the rodeo. If You want me to minister, then You bring them to me." I planned to sit and watch the rodeo. I didn't have a care; it was all on God. Was I in for a shock! From that prayer forth, I was busy ministering as God paraded people by me.

Cowboys would spot me up in the grandstand. They would come get me and say, "I need to talk to you some place where we'll not be interrupted." Cowboys have a lot of pride. They don't want to be seen talking to a minister. We would go off into some of the strangest places you can imagine so they could comfortably talk about Jesus.

The knocks began to be frequent on my camper door, often in the wee hours of the morning when no one else could see them. Many of them were brokenhearted, with tears in their eyes and lips quivering as they confided, "Glenn, I need to talk to you. Do you have the time?"

I'd assure them, "Man, I've got all the time in the world. Come on in." I would open my Bible and say to them, "Thus saith the Lord God."

God had finally gotten me out of the way. It was His ministry, and I was only an instrument He chose to use in the tremendous latter-day outpouring of the Holy Spirit upon professional and nonprofessional cowboys, ranchers, and farmers.

Making myself available and permitting God to use me as He desired, I continued to travel to many rodeos in a reasonable radius from our home in Austin, Texas. The cowboys would actually sit with me in restaurants. I had been a rodeo clown, and they saw I could talk to them about putting a saddle on a bronc or rosin on a bull rope. They accepted me not only as a preacher but as an ex-rodeo professional. Doors of communication were now wide open.

Chapter Four
A NEW BEGINNING

ANN AND I were visiting one evening in the home of Dr. Roy and Gloria Blizzard. It was getting late, and we were having a time of prayer before our departure. Roy was praying. Abruptly he stopped and looked at me. "Glenn, God wants you officially ordained. He says it's time to do it now. I have a friend, Tommy Williams, who pastors Christ's Fellowship Center in Big Spring, Texas. We need to go over there and get you ordained as soon as possible."

Within the next week, Roy called Tommy and made arrangements for my ordination. Shortly, he, Gloria, Ann, and I traveled to Big Spring, where I became an ordained minister of the gospel. Tommy and Jo Ann Williams became personal friends of ours and were used mightily in teaching young converts in the soon-to-come cowboy revival.

I noticed an increased anointing on my life following the scriptural laying-on of hands. Doors began to open. Things began to happen. It was a tremendous relief to simply make myself available to God and see Him work. I found myself accepted in the rodeo world as a representative of Jesus Christ. To me it was a new beginning, or perhaps, the real beginning of the ministry God purposed.

God's next instructions to us were startling: "Sell your home, furniture, and everything that ties you down. Take your family with you on the road full-time. It is the way to obtain maximum results. I will take care of you."

My mind was boggled. I had been asking the Lord in prayer about the difficulty of traveling to and from rodeos and being away from my family so much of the time. However, I was unprepared for His answer. What in the world would we travel in? How would we live? Kay, our youngest, was just entering her sophomore year in school. Physically it appeared impossible. Nevertheless, I was certain I had heard God. He must have a way.

I was reluctant and uncertain about how to approach Ann with my newly acquired heavenly directions. I waited for an opportune time to discuss them with her.

In the interim, we were visiting our pastor, Kenneth Morgan, in his office. Out of the clear blue, Ann commented, "I think God wants us to go on the road as a family. We could sell almost everything and travel in a motor home. Kay could finish high school by correspondence."

Brother Morgan chuckled and said, "That's pretty extreme, Ann. You'd better know that's God before you go out on a limb."

I sat in silent amazement. Once again, God had proved that when He is in on something, He works on both sides. He had jointly prepared our hearts.

We began to pray for a motor home. It was obvious that a mini would not do. We needed one large enough to live in, counsel in, and carry ministry supplies and our personal items. And we did not have one dime to put in it. We figured that if this were truly God's project He'd make the way.

One evening after we had been praying all day, Ann asked me to drive her to the grocery store. Since I'm no grocery shopper, I just pushed the cart and followed her.

We were going down the aisle past the magazine rack. My cart accidentally brushed against several magazines, and one fell to the floor. The name of the magazine was *Motor Home Life*. I stooped down, picked it up, and began to thumb through it. It was full of motor homes and had an article that looked interesting about people who traveled and lived in motor homes. I bought it and took it home.

Reading the magazine, I was staggered at the price tags on the size motor home we needed—fifty to seventy-five thousand seemed to be about average for the top-of-the-line-coaches. I thought, "This is surely going to have to be God."

There was one advertisement for a particular motor home that kept catching my eye. Day after day, after I prayed and studied the Word, I would be drawn back to that magazine. The same ad would grab my attention. I showed it to Ann. It was a picture of a very beautiful motor home with the factory in the background. It appeared to be the ultimate in motor homes and beyond our wildest hopes and dreams. I could not understand why I was repeatedly attracted to that particular ad.

Ann and I went out and began to look at motor homes—mostly used ones—on the local dealership lots.

We would pray, then try to figure out a way we could get one. The only thing keeping us from it was money. The motor home dealers weren't sympathetic to the ministry. They were interested only in selling their product, which is understandable.

We were beginning to get discouraged when God spoke clearly to my heart: "Get in the car and go to that factory you saw in that advertisement. I will work with you to get the motor home."

In obedience to God, Ann and I took our entire worldly fortune, which consisted of forty-eight dollars, and drove almost four hundred miles to the motor home factory.

When we reached there, it did not take long to realize that the Holy Spirit had preceded us and that we were involved in a God-ordained and directed plot.

The only man who could make any major decision regarding a motor home was the designer, founder, and president of this particular motor home company. His secretary told us he was out of the office that day. I assured her if she would look, she would find him somewhere in the building, for I was certain he was there. She was equally certain I was crazy, but finally, to pacify me, she agreed to look.

She returned, looking alternately sheepish and incredulous. With her was a nice-looking fellow with friendly brown eyes and a questioning smile on his face. He offered his hand, and I shook it.

He invited me into his office. (Ann was outside in the car, praying like mad.)

The Lord instructed me to share about our ministry with this distinguished man. He listened attentively. I did not at any time ask him to give me a motor home or even to let me buy one on payments. I just told him the things I thought the Lord would have me say.

I soon discovered that the man was a Christian and deeply loved the Lord Jesus Christ. He said, "Glenn, this may sound funny to you, but the Lord told me a man was coming to talk to me about a motor home, and that this man would be as beneficial to this company as we would be to him. The Lord also has given me a list of questions to ask you."

He asked them, and I answered to the best of my ability. The fellow studied me closely. "Glenn, you are the only minister who has answered these questions to my satisfaction. Come with me."

He led me into another room. There was a large map on the wall. There, this Christian president of the fairly young, class-A motor home factory, outlined to me the areas of the United States in which the company needed their motor homes promoted. It just so happened they were the same areas I needed to travel to promote the gospel!

We agreed, then and there, that in exchange for driving his fabulous motor home I would perform public relations duties for the company in my spare time. What a deal! I was almost beside myself with joy! It was decided that if and when I sold the motor home I was driving, the factory would immediately send me a replacement. They would foot all the insurance and repair expenses. It seemed absolutely too good to be true. And it was, except for God. To say we praised Him on our way home would be to put it mildly!

We went home and sold our furniture and all unnecessary belongings. We placed the money in the bank— about four thousand dollars—to use in our upcoming missionary journey. A year later, a balance of about four thousand dollars was still in that account, and we had traveled an inestimable number of miles and spent considerably more than the original sum.

The most difficult part of our transition was removing Kay from her school and friends. For a time she was resentful. Eventually she adjusted to our new way of life and made new friends. She began to sing at some of our meetings, using the talent God has given her. Pam, by this time, had graduated from high school, had a good job, and was newly married.

We sold our large family car and purchased a little Volkswagen Karmann Ghia. For family transportation it was quite a squeeze. Nevertheless, I we knew we were in the center of God's will.

In retrospect, our first year on the road in the motor home was probably the happiest we had ever known. We left behind many material hindrances and set forth to serve the Lord.

Chapter Five

OPEN DOORS

ODESSA, TEXAS, SEEMED the logical site to initiate our family on the road ministry, seeing it is the first rodeo of each new year. It is also, in our opinion, the coldest and snowiest.

Right off the bat, God gave us favor with the stock contractor and rodeo producer there, Harry Vold, and his family. Interested in spiritual things, Harry soon received Jesus as his personal Lord. He welcomed me into his organization, saying, "I believe that God would have me help you in any way I can." He gave me a job in the arena, where I had the opportunity to get acquainted with every cowboy who came to compete.

At the Lord's direction, I went to a number of the rodeos that Harry had contracted. The Vold Rodeo Company was to be the launch pad for an astounding move of God.

From Odessa, we traveled amid sleet and snow to Denver for the Professional Rodeo Cowboys Association Convention. This is the convention where all the rodeo performers and stock contractors meet with the various rodeo committees to book rodeos, announcers, and clowns and to contract acts for the coming year.

I was sitting, drinking coffee, in the Stouffer Hotel

restaurant when a neatly dressed cowboy walked in, followed on a leash by one of the largest chimpanzees I had ever seen.

I went over to him and introduced myself. I quickly discovered that the chimp was none other than Todo, part of a famous rodeo act. His owner and master, Larry Clayman, was a top rodeo clown and bullfighter. To my amazement, Larry had heard of me. He was a Christian, and he told me, "I am so excited that God has sent someone to the rodeo cowboys."

Before we parted that day, Larry invited me to come to the Springfield, Missouri, rodeo in May and hold a church service in the grandstand. I gladly accepted, recognizing the encounter as one of divine origin.

We traveled hard until May, attending many rodeos. I worked the Vold labor list at most of the rodeos, meeting and befriending cowboy after cowboy. Opportunities were profuse on a one-to-one basis. Walls were crumbling. The cowboys were beginning to be more open. They would stop me if they had a question. It made little difference who was watching. Their wives came to the motor home to seek counsel from Ann regarding personal problems. Barrier after barrier came down.

A meaningful encounter occurred during the Amarillo, Texas, rodeo. Dennis McKinley, a calf roper then residing in South Dakota, came to our motor home to ask questions about the Holy Spirit. We prayed with him, unaware at the time that our paths would cross again and again until they merged into one.

When we pulled into the San Antonio grounds looking for a place to park and plug in our motor home, we were aided by a distinguished looking fellow named Ron Conatser, who motioned us into an empty space next to his white trailer.

He had a beautiful family that included his wife, Jo; son, Jay; and daughters, Tawana, Twila, and Tammy. A strikingly attractive family, the Conatsers were well-known throughout rodeo land. Ron rode saddle broncs, bulldogged steers, and worked various stock contractors. Jo timed rodeos while the girls carried the flags on horseback and did sundry other things. Jay worked alongside his dad, caring for the stock and performing behind-the-scenes duties. They were truly a rodeo family.

Kay was thrilled to find other teenagers traveling the circuit on a full-time basis. The girls became fast friends.

We shared the Lord's Word with the Conatsers occasionally as the Holy Spirit led the way. Ron would watch me intently, saying little. His background was Church of Christ, but he lacked power to resist temptation and had strayed from a childhood commitment to Jesus. I knew, however, that Ron had been taught to highly regard the Word of God. If I could get him to see the reality of Jesus in the now and the power available to us through the Spirit of God, I knew Ron's life would be transformed. I prayed for him daily and was careful to answer his every question with, "The Word of God says..."

I soon discovered that Ron was a sucker for an open

Bible. He would pick it up or read an open passage out of the corner of his eye. I began to leave my Bible open by the chair where he sat when he came into the motor home. I especially concentrated on seeing to it that he was exposed to passages in the Book of Acts regarding the Holy Spirit. As we sat and talked, Ron's eyes would stray to the Bible conveniently placed by his side, and he would soon forget all about our conversation as he became engrossed in the Word. God had begun a work in the Conatser household.

Our needs continued to be supernaturally supplied—often in the most unorthodox ways. We had watched the money we had banked from the sale of our household furnishings dwindle to a low that could have concerned us. We chose to cast our cares on the Lord and to trust Him. Our regular support consisted of two partners and an average monthly total of seventy-five dollars.

In San Antonio, we urgently petitioned the Lord for five hundred dollars and suggested several ways we thought He could supply it. He rejected all of them. One morning I was returning home from my coffee and prayer time, weaving my way through the rodeo traffic. Suddenly, a large car pulled out of nowhere, it seemed to me, and struck my little Volkswagen Karmann Ghia on the fender. The fender was severely crushed. Actually, *demolished* is a more accurate description.

The driver, a San Antonio resident, apologized profusely, assuring me that his local insurance company would make amends quickly. I forced myself to be kind to him as I took the necessary information, all the while thinking, "God, how could You let this happen to me, while I'm out here trusting You like I am?"

Ron Conatser saw my dilemma and appeared with a large sledgehammer. He beat the crumpled car fender in a direction that freed the wheel to turn. The little red car now looked pitiful but could be driven with no problem at all.

The next morning I drove to the office of the insurance agency. Polite and prompt, they issued a check to me for—guess what? That's right, five hundred dollars, which we needed right then. Our car was usable, just not pretty. We rejoiced at God's unusual channel of provision. Within a couple of months He impressed two businessmen to totally fix our car, free of charge.

When we arrived at the Astrodome for the big Houston show, I went into the rodeo office, and the secretary handed me an envelope, addressed to me, postmarked South Dakota. I tore it open. Inside was a check for one hundred dollars from Dennis McKinley. How I thanked God for His time and provision. He was truly taking care of us.

Most of the cowboys thought we were well-heeled because of the elegant motor home God had provided for us. For the most part, they did not know it was factory-furnished and not ours at all. But we believed that God was our sufficiency, who had made us able ministers of His new testament, and with His riches committed to us, we would not lack.

We had a slight interlude in our rodeo schedule in early spring and accepted invitations from the Full Gospel

Businessmen's Fellowship International (FGBMFI) in Roswell, New Mexico. As we entered town we were accompanied and surrounded by a bona fide sandstorm. Roswell looked bleak indeed. We might have fled on the spot if God had revealed to us at that instant that He intended for us to make Roswell our ministry headquarters.

Al Cooper, co-owner of a motor home sales and service outfit, was the affable president of Roswell FGBMFI. The meeting was a tremendous success. People were saved, healed, and delivered. Al and his wife, Tommie, took us under their wing and made us feel at home. The Lord seemed to establish an immediate kinship between us. It was as though we had known each other for many years. Al and his business partner, Ron Jones, performed some vital work on our motor home and car, at no charge. Roswell began to look better.

At the invitation of Dr. Roy Blizzard, we continued on to the West Coast to join him in an appearance on the relatively young Trinity Broadcasting Network, hosted by Paul and Jan Crouch. We appreciated our hosts' far-flung vision (much of which is realized by this time), enjoyed our time with Dr. Roy, and saw our ministry horizon enlarged.

Shortly thereafter, at the Lord's leading, the Coopers offered us a room on the second floor of their business for an office. For the next few years, we used their business address for our mail, and they gladly took and relayed phone message to us on the road. Al became a member of our ministry board, and Tommie, our much-valued secretary. They were there to baby us through the infant years of the ministry—emotionally, mechanically, and financially, on occasion.

Eventually, the Lord directed us into separate paths as we grew and the ministry demanded a larger office space and permanent employees. Al, an electronic genius who worked with the Pentagon in the perfection and installation of microwaves and satellites, was instructed by God to sell his business and build a local Christian television network. He has since successfully done so.

Chapter Six
FIRST CHURCH OF RODEO

Sedalia, Missouri, was an especially beautiful spot in May. The freshness of spring hung in the air, and the old-fashioned rodeo grounds were quaintly attractive. Harry Vold Rodeo Company had contracted both Sedalia and Springfield. We knew we were obeying God by following Harry.

One afternoon, Karen Vold asked Ann if she would keep her daughter, Kirsten, during the performance. Ann was glad to do so, and four-year-old Kirsten arrived on schedule, laden with toys to keep her occupied. While Kirsten played, Ann read the Bible. Periodically Kirsten would look up and ask a question about Jesus. Ann endeavored to answer her in simplicity, remembering Kirsten's age. But Kirsten was persistent. She wanted to know *why* Jesus came, *why* He died, and *what* He was doing now.

Ann was having a struggle, because she didn't want the Volds to think she cornered their daughter the very first time she kept her and forced the gospel down her throat. About that time, Ann reported, the Holy Spirit literally fell in the motor home. She strongly sensed His presence. She knew, then, that God was truly in her conversation with Kirsten and that He desired to minister salvation to a four-year-old child as readily as to an adult.

Ann carefully explained that Jesus, the Son of God, stepped from heaven to earth through the virgin, Mary, and lived a perfect life. He went to the cross at Calvary to shed His sinless blood, which alone can cleanse our sins. She told Kirsten that the Bible declares in Romans 3:23 that "all have sinned, and come short of the glory of God," including little children. She then shared Romans 5:8–9 (paraphrasing the King James Version). "But God commendeth [showed] his love toward us, in that, while we were yet sinners, Christ died for us. Much more then, being now justified [made right with God] by his blood [which alone washes away our sins], we shall be saved from wrath [separation from God forever, and everlasting hell] through him [Jesus and His shed blood]."

Last, Ann shared with Kirsten Revelation 3:20, again simplifying the words: "Behold, I [Jesus] stand at the door [of your heart], and knock: if any man [woman, or child] hear my voice, and open the door, I will come in to him [or her], and will sup [live and fellowship] with him [or her], and he [or she] with me." Ann explained that to open the door of her heart, Kirsten must only ask, out of her own mouth, for Jesus to come in and be her very own Savior and Lord.

Kirsten promptly replied without hesitation, "I want Jesus to live in my heart." Knowing that God had drawn this child to Himself, Ann prayed and led Kirsten in a simple prayer to receive Jesus as her personal Lord.

The rodeo over, Kirsten went home, and Ann fervently hoped that nothing would be said that would be misconstrued by her parents. We were later to learn, through

Kirsten, that she began her Christian walk with true missionary zeal, starting with her parents. As they sat down to dinner that evening, she insisted that they say the blessing. Giving her permission to do so, Harry and Karen bowed their heads. Kirsten began, "Oh, Lord, let us all here know that if we are going to go to heaven, we must ask Jesus to come and live in our hearts…" On and on she preached to her shocked parents. They were understandably silent about the incident for some time.

A couple of days before Sunday, Karen came to me and asked if we would hold a church service then for the crew—Vold Rodeo Company employees and associates. Of course, I gladly did what they asked.

The weather was warm and beautiful, and Karen found a covered pavilion on the grounds that was perfect for our purposes. We set up chairs, and even before the appointed time, I was thrilled and somewhat surprised to see most of the seats filled. I preached a simple sermon on "Jesus Christ, the same yesterday and today and forever" and had everyone bow their heads. I prayed out loud a simple prayer for those who desired to receive Jesus to repeat. I then asked for a show of hands of those who had just invited Him into their hearts. I was amazed to see several hands go up, including Karen Vold's.

Thus was born officially the First Church of Rodeo. From that point on we began to have regular Sunday services at all of the Vold rodeos and many others. Later, Sedalia was the site of a baptismal service. We borrowed a local physician's swimming pool and immersed several of the new converts.

The next week Larry Clayman and Todo the chimp welcomed us as we arrived in Springfield. In fact, they both came into our motor home for something to drink. It seemed a little different to have a big chimpanzee, clothed in western attire, sitting at our table, drinking out of a cup. I noticed that Larry perpetually kept his eyes on Todo, sitting on the edge of his chair. Larry had to be really tough with his chimp, sternly threatening him, to make Todo behave.

Larry's motor home was parked next to ours, and in the daytime he frequently chained Todo outside to a tree. People would come past, picking at him, thinking he was funny. Sometimes they would hold an item out to him, and Todo would dash out, grab it, and climb into the tree, laughing and jeering at them. There was no way for them to retrieve whatever it was. One afternoon a couple kept on and on tempting Todo. I don't know how he did it, but the chimp got the man's boot and scurried gleefully up high into his treetop retreat. The man pleaded, begged, and all but cried, to no avail. Eventually, Larry intervened and forced Todo to relinquish his trophy.

People continually underestimated Todo. While we were at Springfield, Larry took his horse and animal trailer to the factory to be repainted. He left Todo in it, locked in his compartment, and specifically instructed those at the factory to under no circumstances let him out.

We were given the report that some animal-loving soul passed by, saw Todo, and began to play with him. Feeling sorry for him, the man decided to let Todo out of his cage. The entire factory, town, and area soon unitedly regretted the decision. Pandemonium took place.

Todo terrorized the factory. It took him no time to discover the spray paint machines and to paint an assortment of items. He then tried his hand at using the plant's welder. He finally departed the factory and headed to town. Spying a little old lady walking down the street, he picked up a limb and chased her, switching her as she fled as fast as she was able.

A woman was hanging out clothes in her backyard when Todo appeared. He let out her chickens and relocated her laundry to the television antenna on top of her house.

An all-points bulletin went out on Todo. Larry, now back in Springfield, received an urgent call describing Todo's activities. Several alarming hours passed before Todo was subdued and once again incarcerated.

One evening Larry brought his girlfriend, Cindy, to meet us and visit with Ann. Ann showed Cindy through the motor home. When they reached our bedroom, Cindy saw a Bible lying open on the bed. She sat on the bed and fell over on the Bible. "I need Jesus in my heart," she cried. Cindy soon received Jesus as her Lord, and she and Larry were married not long after we departed Springfield. It was continually amazing to us how sovereignly the Spirit of God moved in drawing people to Himself.

Our Sunday service in the Springfield coliseum was a huge success. Clem McSpadden, rodeo announcer, had mentioned it several times during the rodeo, and we had an excellent crowd. Many people came to Jesus that day.

After much prayer, I went to Clem and asked

permission to hold a coliseum service during the National Finals Rodeo (NFR), to be held in Oklahoma City in December. Clem, who headed up the entire NFR, was encouraging and enthusiastic. He promised me the coliseum on the last Sunday of the rodeo. History was in the making! God had truly moved into rodeo.

A precious couple arrived on the rodeo scene while we were in Springfield. Paul and Linda Scholtz had recently graduated from the Assemblies of God Bible College and were seeking their spot in the ministry world. Paul, ordained to the ministry but also a cowboy, brought a horse to the grounds for Harry Vold to try out. He hoped the horse would buck well enough to fit with Harry's string of bucking stock. The horse didn't, but Paul found his niche. He and Linda signed on unofficially with Harry and began to work for the Vold Rodeo Company. They began to sing at our rodeo services, and Paul began to preach as God opened more and more doors.

It was exciting, in July, to be at the daddy of them all—the big Cheyenne, Wyoming, Frontier Days. Things were fairly popping.

Our motor home was full most of the time. Dennis McKinley had reappeared, and with him was a young Spirit-filled cowboy who was the wildest and boldest Christian I'd yet encountered. George Alan Yocham was an excellent calf roper from Bartlesville, Oklahoma, and was overflowing with Jesus. The problem was, he literally terrified the heathen cowboys and girls, and some of the Christians. George Alan had been seen leaping out from behind a wall and screaming, "Repent!" at unsuspecting cowboys visiting in front of a beer stand. On another occasion when he saw an injured cowboy limping along, he offered his services in prayer. When the unbelieving cowboy refused, George Alan did a leap in the air, fluttered his hands, and pranced off chanting, "Suffer, heathen, suffer!" As hilarious as George Alan stories were to us believers, they were equally alarming to unbelievers, who avoid him at all cost.

George Alan's pretty and quiet little wife, Debbie, was just a couple of months pregnant when Ann and I first met them. George Alan, new to the faith walk, decided to claim Mark 11:24 and receive a boy child from the Lord. (Keep in mind that Debbie was already pregnant.) He then announced loudly and frequently to all who would listen (and wouldn't) that Matthew Alan Yocham was on the way. Imagine his dismay and chagrin seven months later when little Jessica Ann Yocham arrived. It took them a while to come up with the name. When he recovered from his despair, George realized that God was not going to change the sex of a child in the womb, that the seed planted would come up. He and Debbie regrouped, and this time claimed the same scripture prior to conception. Within a couple of years, Matthew Aaron Alan Yocham made his debut. George recently confided to us that he was grateful that the Lord didn't overrule natural law and honor his ignorance, because his little girl is so precious to him. I might add that George Alan is remarkably settled these days, although still a glowing Christian.

On one occasion, George Alan really rocked the rodeo world with his bold faith. Every cowboy wants to win at least one go-round at the Houston rodeo. The pay is tremendous, and so is the prestige. George Alan was talking to two heathen cowboys before it was his turn to rope. They were ridiculing his faith in God. George Alan studied them and then announced, "God is really real! You guys watch this run and decide if God is really real." He proceeded to pray while the two looked on in shocked disbelief. He rode into the roping box, smiled up at God, rode out, and roped his calf in the fastest time of the day. The news traveled fast, and from that time on the unconverted cowboys walked an even wider swath around George.

I was working in the Cheyenne arena when I saw a man sitting on the fence wearing a "one way: Jesus" T-shirt. Before I could get to him, he disappeared. Dennis finally rounded him up, brought him to our motor home, and introduced him to Ann and me. He was Larry Smith, a bull-dogger out of Alma, Arkansas, with quite a testimony.

It seemed that Larry had been successful on the professional circuit for many years and then became addicted to drugs and alcohol. For all practical purposes illiterate, Larry had become almost a recluse in his little unfinished cabin on the top of a mountain outside of town. He had become involved in some underworld doings and was reduced to the role of bouncer in a local club.

Desperate, knowing he was dying, Larry cried out to God—if there was one—from his lonely cabin. Jesus, who Larry had no idea existed, appeared to Larry. Without realizing exactly what had happened, Larry was born again and filled with the Spirit of God. He came off that mountain filled with love for everyone and seeking someone who could tell him what had happened. He was supernaturally delivered from both drugs and alcohol.

Larry finally found Christians who would and could scripturally show him what had transpired on the night of his conversion. Larry then once again gave his life to Jesus—a commitment based on the Scriptures. But his salvation, he knew, began that night on the mountain.

Continually trusting the Lord to teach him to read so that he could understand His Word, Larry was immediately concerned for the hearts and souls of his fellow cowboys. He could, at least, share his testimony with them.

The Lord instructed me to give Larry enough money to buy a good leather-bound Bible. He went to town and purchased one. The problem remained: how to read it. Larry began to pray more fervently. Painstakingly, word by word, he began to read. It was not long until Larry could read the Bible fluently, although most other printed matter continued to perplex him. He can now read as well as anyone—a testimony to the tutorage of the Holy Spirit.

No matter how early I arose that year at Cheyenne, Larry was sitting in a chair outside the motor home when I walked out. The questions would begin, and I would answer them until I was almost hoarse. He had an insatiable hunger for the Word and things of God. It was very evident that the call of God was on Larry's life and that God had sent him to me to tutor. I told him all I knew and then maybe some.

Once in a while when I was talked out I would escape

a little while by excusing myself from Larry to go to the public restroom. There I could peacefully sit and pray and think for a while. It usually worked. But one day when I was worn out from questions and announced that I was taking leave to go to the restroom, Larry said, "I'll go with you." We continued our conversation en route. Once there I ducked inside and shut the door. "Good," I thought. "I'll have a few minutes to regroup and to talk to the Lord." No sooner had I thought it when a familiar voice outside said, "Glenn, I've been meaning to ask you about them demons..." I gave up.

Larry went on to become one of the strongest preachers on the rodeo circuit and off. Operating much as an Old Testament prophet, Larry diligently sought God, and it paid off in his life. Soon after we met him he married a lovely girl, Debbie. They traveled down the road with us for the next few years, singing at most of our services.

The first church service we held in Cheyenne was wonderfully well attended, with several decisions to receive Jesus and His love. The Fellowship of Christian Athletes held the final Sunday service in the grandstand with clown Wilbur Plaugher sharing and leading many to the Lord.

Chapter Seven
THE STAGE WAS SET

WE ARRIVED AT Oklahoma City for the 1977 National Finals Rodeo with anticipation and yet a little trepidation. We were exultant that Clem McSpadden had promised us the coliseum for a service on the last Sunday—but would anyone come? The Finals were undoubtedly the social time of the year for rodeo people. The "who's who" in rodeo would be there. To the best of our knowledge, most of them were certainly unaccustomed to having God on the schedule of events. How would the rodeo world react? Once again we cast our fears and doubts on the Lord. We believed that what He had ordained, He would perform.

We parked near the Conatser family, thrilled to see them. Ron was friendly enough, but it wasn't hard to tell that his mind wasn't entirely on the Lord. Jo looked troubled, and later in the evening came to visit with Ann. Ron had disappeared after receiving a mysterious phone call. Jo and Ann had a long talk. Ann shared with her promises from God's Word in regard to her husband and family, her scriptural rights as a wife. Ann assured Jo that God would hasten to perform His Word, if they would believe Him to do so, receive it by faith. They went to the Lord in prayer, agreeing according to Matthew 18:19: "If two of you shall agree on earth as touching any thing that they shall ask, it shall be done for them of my Father which is in heaven."

The change was immediate and evident. When we decided to have a small, outside church service the first Sunday of the Finals, Ron saw to all the details, even finding the place. He and his family comprised most of the attendance. A small handful of shivering folks (it must have been only a little above zero) endured my brief sermon, and if I recall correctly, a couple of them got saved. Thus, our dedicated, if inconspicuous, beginning at the NFR.

Ron continued to demonstrate a hunger for the things of the Lord. He knew that God had some kind of call on his life. He had always known it, even though he had attempted to ignore the Lord. He recognized his need for power and boldness and asked that I pray with him. I'll never forget that day. I laid my hands on Ron and prayed for the Holy Spirit to come upon him, to empower and fill him. I prayed for him the prayer Paul requested in Ephesians 6:19: "And for me, that utterance may be given unto me, that I may open my mouth boldly, to make know the mystery of the gospel." The power of God hit Ron and literally knocked him over against the wall of the motor home. He was saturated with the power of God, and no one who saw him after that doubted it.

But the Lord was setting the stage for a massive out-pouring of His Spirit. Ann and I prayed almost constantly for the upcoming service in the coliseum. I was running scores at each rodeo performance and spreading the word about the service in every way I knew. Clem McSpadden graciously announced the service to the rodeo crowd on Saturday and had it printed in the official rodeo program. We had invited John Mustian, an anointed singer, to provide the music. He and his wife arrived on Saturday, and we discussed the details of the service.

Ann and I retired at nearly 2:00 A.M. on Sunday, absolutely exhausted after a prolonged day of rodeo and ministry. It was freezing outside, and Kay was asleep in the front of the motor home.

We were drifting to sleep when we heard a *rap* on the door. We ignored it, too tired to move and knowing we had to arise early to prepare for the service. A stronger *rap, rap, rap*. Because Kay was asleep in the living room of the motor home, we did not want to let anyone in. We listened quietly.

Whoever was out there refused to be ignored. The *rap, rap* changed to a steady *wham, wham* on our bedroom window and on the side of the motor home. The blows sounded severe enough to cause damage, so I pulled myself out of bed, put on my Wranglers, shirt, and boots, and grabbed a light windbreaker. I went outside.

Under the street light I recognized a man I had met a little earlier in the evening—a man reputed to be a gambler and associated with the mafia. He was also a heavy drinker. During the rodeo he had given me fifty dollars with which to buy Bibles. I had accepted the money and thanked him, hoping he didn't think he was able to buy favor with God.

"Hello, Brad. What can I do for you?" I moved to the back of the motor home and leaned up against it to shield myself from the icy wind. The man was huge, and he was drunk. His speech was severely slurred. He was a crying drunk, and began to rattle incoherently. I tried to make sense out of what he was saying to see if I could help in some way. I couldn't.

Suddenly the big fellow thrust his hand in his pocket and pulled out a huge, and I mean huge, roll of bills and pushed it at me. He mumbled, "Take this for your work for the Lord."

Aware that he was too drunk to realize what he was doing, I said, "Brad, put that up. Someone could knock you in the head for that kind of roll."

He was insistent. He shoved the money at me and demanded that I take it. I knew that when he awoke in the morning he would wonder where his money went. He was too far gone to make a rational decision. Besides that, I could feel the Holy Spirit restraining me from accepting the money. I again refused. It made him mad.

Full of rage, Brad jammed the money back into his pocket. When his hand came out, it was not empty. He was clenching a switchblade knife, which he popped open. The blade gleamed threateningly under the street lamp. "I'm going to kill you, you little S.O.B." Brad stepped toward me. There was no place to go. My back was against the end of the motor home, and I was blocked in by a man twice my size.

"Brad, you can't kill me. I love you. Jesus and I love you." I had barely gotten the words out of my mouth when I saw that he indeed was going to try. He drew back and brought the knife toward my chest full force.

I uttered, "I plead the blood!" The knife came within three inches of my chest and stopped as though it had hit a brick wall. That made Brad angrier. He drew back his arm even further, determined to drive the knife through my chest. I had to make it short: "Jesus, I plead Your blood." Here it came again! Once more, stopping three inches short of my heart. It was as though God dropped a Plexiglas shield between me and the knife. Brad looked thoroughly puzzled as he tried to force it forward. But he wasn't willing to give up. As he again prepared to thrust the knife at me I reiterated, "You can't kill me, Brad. I told you, I love you, and Jesus loves you." I added, "Jesus, I plead Your blood." Cursing me, Brad thrust all his being into making sure that this time the knife would make contact. I thought I could detect a thud as the knife stopped three inches short of my chest.

Brad stopped there, looking bewildered, knife in hand. I pulled myself together and looked at him. "Brad, I command you in the name of my Lord Jesus Christ to leave here. God loves you, and so do I. I am willing to help you in any way I am able, but you leave here now in Jesus' name."

He put the knife in his pocket and turned to leave. A few steps away, he called back over his shoulder, "You'll never have to fool with me again."

I stepped back into the motor home and found Ann sitting straight up in bed. She could not hear anything going on outside, but God had called her to intercession. At first she thought she was praying for Brad's salvation and had endeavored to do so. Yet, to her surprise, she found herself saying, "Satan, I forbid you to cut short my husband's life in the name of my Lord Jesus Christ. I forbid you to touch him. I bind every spirit of murder and violence, as well as every other spirit with an assignment to harm Glenn, and render them powerless in Jesus' name." On and on she prayed until I was safely inside.

We were finally able to sleep after gratefully praising the Lord for foiling the attempt of the enemy. It was evident that God had something in store that made the devil afraid.

Nearing the coliseum that Sunday in 1977, Ann and I could hear John Mustian singing. He had set up early to practice. The closer we got, the harder it was to hold back the tears. The presence of the Holy Spirit was extremely strong, even yards outside of the building. Inside, it was overwhelming. Every inch of the place was saturated with the presence of God. We encouraged John to continue singing until time for the service.

We watched in awe and wonder as people began to arrive. Some of the biggest names in rodeo found their way down to a seat. By 10 A.M. perhaps fifteen hundred people sat awaiting the first official NFR church service, many not knowing what to expect.

We were limited to approximately an hour, so we moved quickly through the music and testimonies. I guess you could call my sermon topic at the first Finals "The Name Above Every Name." The Lord had impressed me to share that even though there were impressive names and credentials in the rodeo world, Jesus had them topped. According to Philippians 2:9–11,

"God also hath highly exalted him, and given him a name which is above every name: That at the name of Jesus every knee should bow, of things in heaven, and things in earth, and things under the earth; And that every tongue should confess that Jesus Christ is Lord, to the glory of God the Father."

At the close of the service I led the crowd in a prayer to receive Jesus as Lord. While their heads were bowed, I asked for those who had received Him for the first time to please raise their hands. Hands flew up all over the place! I would estimate that one hundred and fifty hands were immediately raised, probably more. We urged those who had accepted Jesus to come forward and receive a free Bible. We were swarmed with those doing so, along with others with prayer requests and some just letting us know they appreciated the service. Most people seemed reluctant to leave the building—clinging to the peace and joy that filled the place.

Some months earlier we had purchased the New American Standard New Testaments with a custom designed cowboy cover drawn and donated by Don Hershberger, a saddle bronc rider from Cody, Wyoming. We endeavor to place one in the hands of each new convert; we've given thousands away.

Following the NFR, we stopped to see my mother in Bowie, Texas. The Conatser family, needing a place to park while Ron went to pick up his scoreboard, went with us. Since we had several loads of dirty clothes, Ann decided to go to the laundromat. Jay, Ron and Jo's oldest, offered to drive her. While sorting and folding clothes,

Ann began to talk to Jay about Jesus. In a few minutes she asked him if he would like to receive the Lord. Without hesitation he said that he would. They were going to pray right on the spot, but some well-meaning lady came to help with the clothes. When they got in the car to leave, he bowed his head, prayed, and made Jesus his Lord. Though we were unaware of it then, that was only the beginning of a God-created relationship with Jay. He was chosen by the Holy Spirit for a very special position in our ministry, although it took us a couple of years to discover it.

In 1980, in Cheyenne, Jay came to us. He knew that he had something to do with our ministry but was unable to pinpoint it. We were very hesitant about accepting the responsibility of another person, although we had recently moved from the Coopers's business location to a little townhouse where we used one of the bedrooms as an office. It was the first time in years we had a spot to call home. We could not see how a place with one bedroom could be used to accommodate another person, even though we needed someone to reside permanently at our office. We were also unenthusiastic about committing a set salary to anyone.

Jay understood our misgivings. He only knew that the Lord had shown him that he had a place in our ministry. He assured us he cared nothing about the money. Room and board was all he would expect. He didn't mind sleeping in the motor home or on the couch when we were at home.

We finally agreed that Jay would come to Roswell

on a trial basis. We would furnish room and board and would give him whatever we could weekly after taking out ministry expenses. Fifty to seventy-five dollars was the norm in those early months.

We soon discovered that Jay had a way of quietly, efficiently, and unobtrusively fitting in wherever needed. There was no job too difficult for him or beneath his dignity. He constantly demonstrated concern both for our well-being and that of the ministry. Possessing a keen business head, Jay proved extremely closed-mouth. No prying party could extract a drop of private business or unnecessary information from him. He was scrupulous and trustworthy with funds. We finally awoke to the fact that God had graciously bestowed upon us a helps ministry in the truest sense of the office. Jay stayed to become general manager of Rodeo Cowboy Ministries, later to become International Western World Outreach Center.

Chapter Eight
HERE COMES THE RAIN

THE LOGICAL PLACE to go after San Antonio was Houston. I had never considered doing anything else. After all, Houston was one of the bigger rodeos, and one could catch nearly any cowboy there at one time or another. Yet, the Spirit of God began to stir within me, mentioning Tucson, Arizona. I did not want to go to Tucson. Houston was only about two hundred miles away. Tucson was many hundreds. I persisted in planning to go to Houston.

During my early morning prayer and Bible study time, God once again brought up Tucson. I prayed, "Father in heaven, if You are directing me to Tucson, I will go. I don't want to, but I will if it is You. Some way, Lord, out of Your Word, give me specific leading, and I will do it." I continued to pray as I read different passages in my Bible. Within a few minutes the Lord had convinced me through Scripture to "go to the west." Tucson it was.

Ann, Kay, and I arrived in Tucson and for three days wondered why we were there. On the fourth day a leading calf roper, Willard Moody, came to our motor home. Willard—four times a National Final Rodeo qualifier—was deeply concerned about the spiritual welfare of one of his best friends, a very well-known roper. Willard wanted us to tell him how to help his friend and began to describe the man's state. Willard and I were sitting on the couch, and Ann stood at the sink washing the dishes.

She had been very quiet. Suddenly, she interrupted our conversation. "Glenn, God keeps telling me that Willard is a dead man."

"No, Ann. Willard wants to help his friend." I tried to ignore her.

She wouldn't be put off. "God is telling me over and over that Willard is dead." She was speaking of being dead spiritually, but Willard didn't know that. His eyes got as big as saucers and a little wild looking.

Ann looked at Willard and began to tell him some things to tell his friend, like the necessity of receiving Jesus as his personal Lord and that one could not get to God apart from Jesus, who alone had made atonement for our sins. Willard put up his hand and stopped her. "Whoa! I don't know what you are talking about."

Ann looked at him and smiled. "I know you don't. God has brought you here, Willard, to save you."

By this time I had come to my senses. It was clear why we were in Tucson. God, in His perfect timing, had crossed Willard's path with ours for him to hear about God's demonstrated love in sending Jesus. I carefully went through scripture after scripture showing Willard the fall of man, the necessity of redemption, and the love of our Savior, who stepped from heaven to earth to shed His sinless blood in payment for the sins of lost humanity. I told him that man must verbally accept the free redemption that Jesus accomplished at Calvary, reading to him Romans 10:13: "For whosoever shall call upon the name of the Lord shall be saved."

Willard stated in amazement that never in his life had he heard or understood the things we shared with him. He took off his hat, bowed his red-haired head, and sincerely invited Jesus to become Lord of his life as I led him in prayer. He joyously departed, immediately beginning to witness to his travel buddies.

We had met with Willard by divine arrangement. "I have a call on this man's life to preach the gospel," God spoke as I prayed for Willard. Sure enough, within a few months Willard was elected as the next president of the Cowboy Chapter, FCA. Within a couple of years I was privileged to preach his ordination service, which included the scriptural laying-on of hands. Willard pastored a church in Oklahoma for a while, then was called by the Lord back into an evangelistic teaching ministry.

Tulsa, Oklahoma, has been the site of some unusual and exciting happenings in the rodeo world. We have held several church services in the coliseum during the Johnny Wills Stampede. One, in particular, was a little different.

Right before the service, a car pulled up to the entrance of the coliseum, and a drunken Native American man staggered out. With slurred speech he announced that Dennis McKinley had invited him the evening before to come to cowboy church on Sunday. Although he had been out partying all night, he remembered the invitation. Thoroughly intoxicated, the man was a mess. His clothes were bloodstained and filthy. He had undoubtedly been fighting as well as drinking. He stood there, reeling to and fro, clutching a six-pack of beer under one arm.

We hastily rounded up Dennis and George Alan Yocham. They induced the Native American man to leave his six-pack outside and escorted him into the church service. Sitting on the second or third row, they placed him between them, and we began the service. Almost from the moment he sat down, the fellow slumped over, apparently asleep or unconscious.

We breezed right through the singing and a couple of testimonies without a hint of trouble. The guy slept right through them. I stood up to preach. The anointing and presence of God in the coliseum was tremendous. I began to share the love of a living Savior with a rapt audience. Their faces told me that many of them had never heard of God's concern and provision for them, personally.

Suddenly, the man straightened up, thrust out his arm, and intoned loudly, "Bless my mother, bless my father, and all of these. Amen." He then slumped to his seat, his head on his chest. Glancing at Dennis and George Alan, I endeavored to recapture my train of thought and went on with my sermon—temporarily. In two or three minutes the man once again came alive and pronounced an even louder blessing on more people. This time I glared at Dennis and George Alan. They were both looking right at me, grinning from ear to ear as if to say, "What do you want me to do?" I can still see George's white teeth shining as I struggled to regain my composure.

I proceeded from where I thought I had left off, and all went well for the next three or four minutes. This time the fellow really got involved. He very vocally blessed several people and then began to confess his sins, one by one.

I finally recognized that the enemy was using this poor, unsuspecting man in an attempt to totally wreck our church service. I got mad, not at the man, George Alan, or Dennis but at the devil. I began to pray. I took authority in the name of Jesus over the spirits that were controlling the person and rendered them powerless in His name. I believed God for the man's freedom and salvation. As I ended by prayer, he took a deep breath and became silent. He remained that way until the end of the service. In spite of the interruptions, at the close of the meeting when I gave the invitation many responded to receive Jesus, and God got the victory!

On another occasion in Tulsa, God demonstrated His power to a packed crowd of several thousand in the coliseum. A bareback bronc rider came out of the chute on a wildly bucking horse. Trouble lay ahead for the young man. Within a few moments he bucked off across his hand. That means his body went across his hand that was in the rigging, placing his head by the horse's kicking feet. As the crowd watched and gasped in horror, blood began to trickle and then gush from the young man's head. The horse circled the arena over and over as the rider dangled helplessly. In vain, the pickup men tried to rescue him. Many in the crowd became ill just watching. One woman suffered a heart attack and had to receive first aid.

It was one of the worst calamities I had personally witnessed in a rodeo arena. For what seemed an interminable amount of time, the horse's feet thrashed the head and upper body of the contestant. Finally, as his very life ebbed away, the boy's hand slid lifelessly out of the rigging, and he lay, a mutilated heap, in the arena dirt.

"Go lay hands on the young man. Pray for him, and I will raise him up." I had no doubt I was hearing the voice of the Lord. He was clear and distinct. Scarcely hesitating, I ran to the young rider. To my surprise, another figure arrived at the boy's side, perhaps two steps ahead of me. It was Dennis McKinley; God had spoken to him also.

A close view of the rider was not faith-inspiring. The aura of death was upon him. His fingernails had turned a bluish color. He appeared to be absolutely lifeless, all breath gone. Dennis and I placed our hands upon him and began to pray with intensity. We pleaded for his life, claiming every scripture pertaining to healing and God's grace that we could recall. We spoke life to his limp form. Glancing down at his hands, we saw that his color was returning. We prayed harder. The very life of God permeated the young man's body until his tone was normal. Wounds began to heal and close in front of our very eyes! Within a few minutes the cowboy sat up and asked what he was doing there. He looked at himself incredulously. He had been made every whit whole! We could only weep, giving glory to God for such a manifestation of His love and power.

Looking behind us, we noted that the ambulance had screeched to a halt, and the entourage accompanying it was watching God's medicine administered in open-mouthed amazement. That day in Tulsa there was not a doubt—even in the heathens' hearts—that God had visited the rodeo with a miracle.

Chapter Nine
WHEN IT RAINS IT POURS

N 1978 AND 1979, Cheyenne, Wyoming, was the scene of a tremendous outpouring of the Spirit of God. I don't think I have personally witnessed anything like it, even until the present.

Aside from our usual services, we had teaching sessions in one of the big horse barns every night. There, on makeshift bleachers, out behind stalls filled with blanketed horses, God met with us in a mighty way. The Christians would often bring someone with them who didn't know Jesus. Others stopped in simply out of curiosity, and quite by accident it seemed to them, met the living Savior.

Cowboys and girls would spontaneously leap to their feet and give their testimonies. There is something indescribably special about a big tough cowboy wearing a championship buckle standing there telling all his friends and everyone who will listen what Jesus means to him, how God has changed his life. Eventually, after the testimonies subsided, I would preach the Word.

One night I was preaching (it was almost 11:30 P.M.), and no one showed signs of wanting me to stop. We were having a wonderful time in the Lord. As I walked and talked I glanced toward the back of the barn. There stood Roy Duvall looking mighty serious. I knew by the way

Roy fixed his eyes on me that something was bothering him badly and that he could hardly wait until I got through preaching to talk to me. I had an uneasy feeling in my spirit that maybe I had said something that offended him, and he had come over to settle the score, so to speak. A champion steer wrestler, Roy is one of the largest men I have ever met and topping his size was his reputation as a fighter.

After I closed the service, I began to pray for the sick. Several of the cowboys who had injured legs and knees came for prayer. The power of God was there to heal. We saw Him do absolute miracles that night. Roy waited until the prayer line diminished and then came over to me. He pointed his finger right between my eyes and announced, "*I want to talk to you'n out behind the barn.*" At such close range, I was especially awed by his enormous size. Before I could turn to follow him, he grabbed me with his right arm and began to drag me out of the barn. I thought, "What a shame to get my head bashed in when God is doing such exciting things out here."

Everyone stood as if transfixed and watched Roy escort me out behind the barn. I am sure their minds, like mine, thought the worst. They knew Roy's reputation too. I must have looked a pathetic sight, my head barely reaching the underside of Roy's huge arm.

Once outside the barn, Roy's voice broke. "I don't want you to ask God for anything for me, but I want you to ask Him to heal my horse."

I breathed a sigh of relief and calmly asked, "What is wrong with him?" I was aware that the horse Roy spoke of was part of his famous and extremely valuable bulldogging team, by which he and his wife, Karen, made a large part of their yearly income.

"Well, the vet said that he is so foundered that he might not even make it through the night. He is very sick. I want you to pray for him. I believe if you do, God will heal him."

It was pouring down rain. Yet, I needed to stall for a little time to have a short conversation with God. I said, "Roy, I'll do it. Get him and bring him here." While Roy was gone, I pleaded with God, "Father, please touch this horse. Please don't let me down."

Roy returned with his horse, and I fervently laid my hands on him. I began to pray, "Father, in the name of Jesus..." I didn't even get to finish my prayer. The power of God instantly touched the horse, causing him to leap backward several steps. He was miraculously healed, and we both knew it.

There were some other cowboys outside feeding their horses. They saw us praying for Roy's horse. I'm sure they thought, "Boy, this is the nuttiest thing I have ever seen." But Roy didn't seem to care who saw us. He was a happy man. He could see that God had healed his horse, and he put him back in the stall and fed him. As he came back to the trailer to put his feed bucket up, the Spirit of the Lord spoke to me and said, "Ask him what is keeping him from giving his life to Me right now."

I began to talk to Roy about the love of Jesus. I asked, "Roy, what is keeping you from giving your life to the Lord?"

He hesitated, then answered, "Just me, I guess."

I kept on, "Roy, wouldn't you like to receive Jesus tonight?"

He softly replied, "Yes, I would. But I want Karen to be there. Let's go to my camper." We walked across the parking lot and got into his camper, where Karen awaited us. She had been praying for Roy and felt that somehow this was to be the night her prayers were answered. And so it was! As I led Roy in the sinner's prayer he genuinely committed his heart and life to the Lord Jesus Christ.

Before the break of day the news had spread throughout the rodeo grounds that Roy Duvall had "gotten religion." To confirm their suspicions, Roy was seen early in the morning preaching to some of his friends. While they sat and leaned on a flatbed truck, Roy walked to and fro, preacher style, his handkerchief in his hand. He was telling them what he had done, telling them they needed Jesus in their lives. One of them was heard to say, "Damn right, Roy." They weren't about to cross their fearless leader!

That very day, Roy took his horse to a rodeo in Colorado, rode him, and won the bulldogging.

God made His intentions clear there in Cheyenne. He desired involvement with the cowboys and their possessions, which, of course, included their beloved livestock. What better way to demonstrate His love for them than to heal their valuable animals?

Willard Moody's horse, Charlie, one of the finest roping horses on the circuit, had become very sore in the withers and legs. When Willard heard about Roy's horse, he came and asked me if I would pray for Charlie. We prayed for him, and God healed him. Before long, the cowboys were noticing. "Hey, the preachers are praying for those horses," they would tell one another. "God is doing something. He must be real!" We rejoiced at the unique ways God gained the attention and respect of the cowboy world—and at the souls that were coming to Him because of His revelation of love.

Ann and I barely were able to gain enough privacy to tell each other good morning or night. We were so engrossed in counseling and ministry. During these years at Cheyenne, actual lines would form outside our motor home as individuals and couples awaited their turns. They sat in lawn chairs, on car fenders, or on the ground. Regardless of the hour, God met their needs.

In one of these prayer lines, awaiting entrance to our motor home was a young, recently married couple who were regulars on the rodeo circuit. The man was an excellent bareback rider, and we were fond of them both. As they sat on the couch, they shared their problem, which seemed insurmountable to them, but they were willing to believe that God could solve it. It was a matter of money. They were out. Ann and I ministered to them along the lines of faith and the trustworthiness of God's Word. You could see from watching their faces that they had very little revelation along these lines but were eager to believe. We bowed our heads to pray and believe God for a financial miracle. As we did, the Spirit of God spoke to my heart: "Give them one thousand dollars." He was explicit. "But God, the only money we have to speak of is that one thousand dollars that we are saving to print more Bibles," I silently argued.

Very reluctant to part with the money saved for such an important purpose, I attempted to debate with that voice. He didn't budge an inch. I withdrew my arguments and prayed the prayer of faith for the couple. Then I stood up and walked to the drawer where we kept our checkbook. As I wrote out the check, three sets of eyes were fastened on me. Ann's were especially expressive. She knew that the only money in that account was our Bible money, and we had considered it untouchable for any other purpose.

I handed the check to the young bareback rider. "I give you this in the name of Jesus." Incredulously, they looked at one another, overwhelmed almost to the point of tears. Their facers flooded with relief and joy. They thanked us and left.

Little did I know what point the Lord desired to make through that gift. We were oblivious to the fact that many of the unsaved (and some of the Christian) cowboys and girls thought that all preachers, including us, were out for their money, and watched us suspiciously. The news of what the preacher had given one of their companions covered the circuit like wildfire. Afterward we were treated with a new respect by many of those who had previously avoided us. God had removed another barrier between them and His love.

To top it off, He also immediately affected His promise in Luke 6:38: "Give, and it shall be given unto you; good measure, pressed down, and shaken together, and running over, shall men give into your bosom. For with the same measure that ye mete withal it shall be measured to you again." Cowboys and girls and people we hardly knew came to us at all hours bringing sizable gifts. We left Cheyenne with several thousand dollars, praising God for His laws of increase. We had enough, not only for our Bibles, but also to give to some of the others the Lord had recently called to minister in the cowboy world.

We first met Earl and Pam Acton at Cheyenne. A ranching couple from Ozona, Texas, they were parents of twins, Marty and Bobbie, and rodeoed periodically when they could get away from the ranch. On one occasion, when our financial standing looked bleak by physical sight, a check arrived in the amount of sixty-eight hundred dollars. It was the tithe off of the twins' lamb, which had just won grand champion at Houston. How we praised God for His provision and for the unselfishness and obedience of the twins.

Kenny and Glenda McMullan were also part of our early rodeo family in the Lord. Glenda was, perhaps, one of the earliest converts, realizing that her own goodness and morality were not sufficient to get her to heaven. A tall, attractive, and genuinely unassuming ranch girl, Glenda, to put it mildly, was bold in the Lord. Outspoken and without guile, Glenda approached life and all encountered in it head-on. She said what she thought needed to be said, and she asked what she wanted to know.

Studying the Word avidly and filled with the Spirit

of God, Glenda, even though a young Christian, became convinced of her position and authority in the Lord Jesus and His name. One day she was traveling the back roads in the middle of nowhere, in the area near Iraan, Texas, where she and Kenny live and ranch. She came upon a camper and pickup parked in the road, and a scene of hysteria. A man was threatening a woman and another person with a gun. Glenda jammed on her pickup brakes, jumped out, and confronted the group. She demanded in the name of Jesus that the man drop the gun—which he did, both startled and stunned. In her forthright manner, she straightened the group out, climbed back into her pickup, and proceeded on her way.

Accompanying us on an Israel tour, Glenda was a breath of fresh air to us personally and, I believe, to all those in our group, as well as the native Israeli. Our guide took a personal liking to her, for she asked question after question (many of which others would have liked to ask but were too dignified to do so) in child-like curiosity accompanied by extreme intelligence. One shocker: When we arrived at the Israeli-guarded Syrian border, Glenda got out of the tour bus to take a picture. Asking another tourist to take a picture of her, she moved to one of the soldiers, removed his helmet, and put it on. Then she helped herself to his machine gun and cheerily posed for her picture while the soldier (whom she graciously included in her picture) was transfixed in startled disbelief. After she returned his gun and helmet, the soldier began to laugh, as did his colleagues. Her lack of intimidation brought shock and successive joy to many.

Kenny had received the Lord without fanfare in the bleachers during "slack" at an Amarillo, Texas, rodeo. A good man, it took a little time for Kenny to realize his need for salvation. Kenny's calf-roping horse, Lemonade, developed some severe problems during the Cheyenne rodeo. Two vets had looked at him and had given a serious diagnosis, cautioning Kenny not to ride him. Now Kenny was entered in the calf roping, and Lemonade was the only horse he had with him. Yet, the horse's leg was wrapped and full of fever.

As I stood looking at the horse, I heard the Spirit of the Lord say to me, "Pray for the horse, and I will heal him right now."

I said, right in front of the veterinarians, "Kenny, I am going to lay hands on your horse and pray for him, and God is going to heal him for you right now so that you can ride him."

Kenny replied, "That's good, boy. Let's do it now."

I laid hands on the horse and began to pray. After I had prayed the prayer of faith I said, "Kenny, according to the Word of God your horse is healed and made whole in the name of Jesus Christ."

Everybody standing there looked at me as though I were some kind of nut. Yet, Kenny knew in his heart that his horse was healed. He began to act in faith. (Faith without works is dead. See James 2:17.) He said, "If he is healed, I don't need this wrap on his leg anymore." He took out his knife and began to cut the wrap off the horse's leg. As he did so he announced to the vets, "I believe you men have done all you know to do, but I believe that God has healed my horse. One of you feel and see if the fever is gone."

They felt all over the horse, and one of them looked at the other in amazement and said, "There is no fever in this horse whatsoever."

Some of the cowboys who were standing around there that day have come to know the Lord Jesus just because of God's grace and healing power demonstrated to Kenny and his horse.

At the same rodeo, Kenny's nephew, Dean, had a horse that was experiencing severe colic. He was having a terrible time with him, and the vet was very concerned about him. One morning at about two o'clock, I heard a knock on the door. "Get out here in a hurry," a frantic voice called. Quickly dressing, Ann and I both hurried out to view a very worried cowboy with his horse. He was up in the roping next day, and his horse had a bad case of colic. You could see and almost feel the pain that horse was in.

Dean said, "I want you to pray for this horse." Ann and I laid our hands on him, anointing him with oil. The only oil we had was liquid cooking oil. Even before I said, "Amen," we could feel the relief in the horse—all because we prayed in the mighty name of Jesus.

Again the veterinarians were astonished. One said to me, "If you Christian cowboys don't quit laying your hands on these horses and praying for them, you're going to put me out of business." I assured him that was definitely not our intent. We were there strictly to magnify the Lord Jesus Christ.

You can imagine their amazement when the cowboy rode the horse the next day and won several thousand dollars on him. The news that God had healed another horse flew throughout the circuit.

At Cheyenne, as well as many of the other rodeos, we began to hold baptismal services, immersing new converts. The Cheyenne motel Little America has been the scene of numerous baptisms. Usually a good crowd of believers would appear to applaud their new brothers and sisters as they followed Jesus in scriptural baptism. In wintertime, we have endeavored to find motels with enclosed pools. For most part, the management has been courteous and cooperative in permitting us to use their facilities. On occasion, when necessitated, we have used stock tanks and icy cold creeks. Once in a while, a kindly pastor has invited us to use his church baptismal, no strings attached.

We have also endeavored to serve the Lord's Supper to groups of believers as often as possible, though we avoided doing so in the large coliseum church services where so many attending are unsaved.

We had arrived at the 1979 Cheyenne rodeo a few days early. Parked and plugged in on the rodeo grounds, Ann was typing feverishly, trying to finish a pamphlet or booklet of some sort. I was working, doing something outside the motor home, when her electric typewriter went dead. Thinking I had unwittingly unplugged the electricity, she bolted outside to correct the matter. I directed her attention to the sky, which had been turbulent all day long. Coming directly at us, say a block or so away, was a mammoth black tornado. Stop signs, roofs, and all kinds of debris filled the air. It was eerie.

Knowing that Jesus had given us authority over all the power of the enemy according to Luke 10:19, we put into practice what we believed and what we preached. With the huge vacuum almost upon us, we spoke loudly. We spoke repeatedly, and we spoke in faith. We rebuked the tornado in the name of Jesus, commanding it to be removed, to turn, forbidding it to come near us. Mark 11:23 became a greater reality to us that day. Jesus promised, "For verily I say unto you, That whosoever shall say unto this mountain, Be thou removed, and be thou cast into the sea; and shall not doubt in his heart, but shall believe that those things which he saith shall come to pass; he shall have whatsoever he saith." Ann held up her Bible, which she had brought outside with her, pointing to and claiming Psalm 91 over us and our possessions. We both felt charged with the Spirit of God, all fear held at abeyance.

As we spoke the unalterable Word, which promised our protection, we witnessed the ugly whirling monster bow its knee to the sovereign name of Jesus and His authority. Almost abruptly, it turned, choosing a path perpendicular to the rodeo grounds. We watched, praying for others, as it ravaged a large part of Cheyenne.

Along with a few of the Christians who had also arrived early for the rodeo, we had a praise session that night, thanking God for His delivering power. I couldn't resist teasing Ann a little, telling her that Jesus told us, "Whatsoever shall *say* to the mountain," not *scream*, as she had been doing.

Chapter Ten

AH, LORD GOD! NOTHING IS TOO HARD FOR THEE!

WE CONTINUED TO establish, under the leadership of the Holy Spirit, Sunday services at almost every rodeo to which we traveled. Some of the rodeo committees were very cooperative—others, gospel hardened. In that case, when the coliseum or arena bleachers were denied us, we made do by using bales of hay for seating the congregation, simply setting up our service in some spot outdoors on the rodeo grounds. The music and preaching would draw many who would never have come even into the grandstands. Can of beer in hand, a really tough one would hang around just long enough for Jesus to hook him and, slumping down on a bale, head bowed, he would pray to receive the Lord. Some of the strongest converts just happened to bump into Jesus in such a manner.

We traveled through Washington State, ministering on new terrain to us. The Ellensburg committee was extraordinarily cooperative, giving us the grandstands for our services and seeing to it that they were announced frequently to the rodeo crowd.

We had a family on the circuit who had a cute little girl, Heather, who owned a huge Doberman. The dog's name was Rocky, and he had been kicked by a horse so severely that his leg was withering. The vets didn't know what to do with him, apparently. They had just let him go, and instead of getting better he daily got worse. Heather had heard that we prayed for horses and came to me and asked if I would pray for Rocky. I assured her that I would the next time that I saw him, and then forgot all about it.

Ann and I had been over at the Ellensburg rodeo office to use the phone and were returning to our motor home to get ready for the performance. All around were cowboys saddling their horses and preparing to compete. Suddenly, Heather appeared, wanting me to pray for Rocky. I again assured her that I would when I saw him. Delighted, she screamed, "Here he is. Here's Rocky. Pray for him now!"

My first reaction was, "Oh, dear God, no. Not in front of all these people." It seemed the most confirmed unbelievers were those around us right then. Yet, Ann and I knew we had to pray. Heather was counting on us, and I was counting on her faith to bail us out.

I told Ann to put her hands on the withered leg end, while I put mine on the biting end, and we knelt beside the big dog. He stood there, panting with his tongue out on his three good legs. The other one dangled uselessly, appearing very pitifully shrunken at close range. My faith was not at an all-time high. I hoped Ann's was. We shut our eyes, and I began to pray, beseeching God to intervene on Heather's behalf and heal her dog. To my dismay, I heard the shuffle of boots as cowboys stopped what they were doing and moved over to see the *show*.

I prayed as fervently as I was able in such a situation.

Eyes still closed, I ended my prayer of faith and came to the realization that the space under my hand was vacant. I moved my hand all around. No dog was there. I opened my eyes. There lay Rocky, vibrating on the ground, obviously slain in the Spirit. The little crowd looked on in astonishment while God performed a healing on Rocky that was second to none. In a few moments, he was up and off on all four legs, a testimony to God's love, grace, and mercy.

Every day in Ellensburg the Christians gathered to pray for lost souls. Willard Moody had a friend with him to whom he had been witnessing for three days. Richard was almost to the point of being hardened to the gospel. Very well-known in the western world, his life was a major wreck. The devil almost had him convinced that he was beyond God's help.

One night we had eighteen people packed inside our motor home for a communion service. A knock came on the door. It was Willard. He said, "I have Richard here, and I believe if you will talk to him a few minutes, he will give his life to Jesus."

I went outside and asked him, "Would you like to receive Jesus as your Lord and Savior?"

"I don't know. I kind of would, but I'm not sure it would work for me," he answered.

I talked with him briefly. After a few minutes I could see he wasn't persuaded, so I decided to use shock tactics. I said, "You can either receive Jesus right now and through Him receive eternal life, and He will straighten your life out for you, or you can die and go to hell. You don't have any other choice. And it is not Jesus' fault if you die and go to hell."

Richard grabbed my shirt. "Wait a minute. They didn't put it to me like that." He came into the motor home, and within a few minutes Richard Stowers was a new creature in Christ. He was a key figure in God's early move among cowboys, because most of them figured that if God could and would save Richard, He could do anything. His fighting reputation was legendary and seldom exaggerated. Anyone who crossed him desperately needed God's immediate help.

Richard bore scars that day from his most recent conflict with his wife, Joyce. Their home was a genuine battleground, and if Richard had feared anyone or anything, it would have been Joyce. When angered, she attacked with anything available. One time she cut off all his Wranglers when he planned to leave for a rodeo she felt unnecessary.

So, of course, as we counseled with him, his immediate concern was about Joyce. Their relationship was not exactly one of mutual trust, and he wondered how she would react.

Loaded down with tapes, a recorder, a Bible, and other material, Richard returned home. Joyce met him at the airport, and on the way home he related to her what happened to him in Ellensburg. She watched him warily.

A few weeks later, at Albuquerque, Richard brought Joyce to meet us. A tall, beautiful girl, Joyce, very obviously, was not a weak-willed individual. Ann and I immediately thought what a great Christian she would make. To insure privacy, we went to the hotel where

Richard and Joyce were staying. Ann ministered to Joyce in one room, while Richard and I prayed and waited in another. In a no-nonsense matter, Joyce asked questions. When satisfied, she desired to receive the Lord, and they prayed. Then Ann shared with her God's attitude toward her family life and prayed again with her. To Richard's delight and amazement, Joyce didn't prove a hard case at all for God. When she later received the baptism of the Holy Spirit, Joyce became a powerhouse for the Lord and a prayer warrior who settled for nothing less than what the Word of God promises.

No doubt, the Stowerses' conversion made more of an impact on lives who knew them than anyone would dare estimate.

Shortly after Richard's Washington encounter with Jesus, Rick Bradly, a world-champion steer wrestler, came to us to request prayer for his injured ankle. Severely twisted and damaged, the ankle was a tremendous hindrance to Rick's bull-dogging skill. We (several of the Christian cowboys) laid hands on the ankle and watched God perform an absolute miracle of healing. Rick demonstrated the healing, joyously, to all who would look or listen.

THE WORD SPREADS

Aware that we now had a mobile church on our hands, Ann and I were concerned about feeding the new converts, as well as those who had recommitted their lives to the Lord. Knowing that only a diet of truth from God's Word would make them strong, driving out and preventing error, we made our concern a matter of prayer. The Lord answered in unique ways.

Bob and Mary Ann Rowan, the couple who manned our first office—if you could call it that—in Austin, Texas, were sensitive to the voice of the Lord. Needing to dispose of some tithe money, they sought the Lord. He distinctly impressed them to buy a few dozen tape recorders and to give them to me. At first I couldn't figure out what was going on. What in the world was I going to do with all those tape recorders? Then it dawned on me! As the cowboys and girls traveled (boy, did they travel!) they could listen to tapes from reputable ministers on the recorders. When they met at various rodeos, they could exchange their tapes for others, thus, keeping the tapes in circulation. Our motor home would house the tape library.

We joyfully took the recorders and began to pass them out. We were thrilled with the Lord's ingenuity. Most of the cowboys and girls would not, at this point, have thought or even known to get a recorder. For the most part, they had no idea that teaching tapes on the Bible were available. But when placed in their hands, they would certainly listen. We began our tape distribution with some of the teaching tapes Ann and I listened to and a few tapes of my own sermons, which had been recorded when I had occasionally ministered in churches. It was obvious from the hunger of our "congregation" that more tapes were soon to be desperately needed. As usual, God was ahead of us.

Brother Kenneth and Gloria Copeland were ministering at Lakewood Church, pastored by Brother John

Osteen, in Houston during a Thanksgiving convention. Ann and I were attending, just absorbing the Word in an effort to refuel. We both felt spiritually drained. Tommy and JoAnn Williams were there also for the same purpose and invited us to go with them to lunch at the hotel where many convention guests were staying.

As we sat enjoying our meal, Brother Kenneth and Gloria walked in. To date, we had never personally met them, although we felt we knew them through Mr. and Mrs. A. W. Copeland, Kenneth's parents. Passing our table, they stopped to greet Tommy and Jo Ann, who, in turn, introduced us. Brother Kenneth kindly expressed his delight in meeting us, saying he had heard much about us from his mother. He asked several questions about our ministry, displaying genuine interest. Before he walked away, he turned and said, "Glenn, I want to have a part in your ministry. I want you to stop by my tape table and pick up copies of every tape I have with me." (I had told him how the cowboys listened to tapes going down the road.) He said he would leave instructions with a particular employee. Thanking him profusely, we rejoiced at God's timing as well as His continuous provision.

Taking Brother Kenneth at his word, we later stopped by his tape table, where, sure enough, his employees had prepared several boxes—several enormous boxes—of tapes. Thrilled, we stowed them in our motor home and soon had them in circulation.

But God wasn't through yet! Only a few months later we returned to Houston for the rodeo. Low on funds, we needed a visible miracle in order to continue our travels and told God so. After the cowboy church service, we invited several of our Christian cowboys and girls to go with us out to Brother John and Dodie Osteen's church for the evening service.

Brother John and Dodie greeted us so very graciously. He had asked that I share with his congregation a bit about God's dealings with cowboys. As I stood on the platform facing that sea of faces, I remember thinking, "I don't think I'm ready for this." Thank God for Dodie's marvelous sense of humor and sensitivity. She mercifully turned the lights out on me a couple of times, and as we joked, I felt much more at ease. Having shared a couple of incidents to a warm and responsive congregation, I sat down.

Brother John preached a short, power-packed sermon in his very own inimitable style, gave an invitation, ministered to those in need, and prepared to close. He stopped short and looked at me. "Brother Glenn, Dodie and I want to be a part of your ministry. We want to help. I want to give you a copy of every one of my tapes and books for you to distribute as you see fit." He then instructed his people to prepare the boxes. He and Dodie proceeded to bless us with a check for five hundred dollars.

As we loaded box after box of Brother John's tapes and books, we could only praise God for the Osteens' missionary heart and sensitivity to the Spirit of God. Both his and Brother Kenneth's tapes and literature meant more to the continuation of the cowboy ministry than I could possibly describe.

We had already composed and printed cowboy-geared tracts, as well as printed the New American Standard New Testament with a cowboy cover. It now seemed that the Lord was talking to us about printing a newsletter. We were ignorant but willing. He gave the name: *The Conqueror.* We were to include a brief teaching, testimony, and a personal column to our partners and friends under the title "Behind Chute 7."

Enjoying the task of writing, Ann labored over our first issue, securing cowboy interviews, typing one of my sermons, and cornering me for my personal column. Soon the first four-page edition of *The Conqueror* emerged. It has become a bimonthly publication of eight pages in recent years, and through it the Spirit of the Lord ministers to a mass of western oriented homes as well as to others. We have been exceedingly blessed by the artwork of Don Hershberger, whose lifelike pictures adorned the cover of *The Conqueror,* as well as our New Testaments, tracts, and mini-books.

THE WOLVES CAME

Paul warned in Acts 20:29, "For I know this, that after my departing shall grievous wolves enter in among you, not sparing the flock."

Various types of very different people had come to me announcing that they were sent to minister to the cowboys. Most of them stayed around a little while and drifted off. One fellow was really enthusiastic over the prospect of being a cowboy preacher. He queried me about a variety of things, including finances. "How much does it pay?" He eyed our motor home, obviously thinking we weren't doing badly.

"It pays however much you need and want," I replied.

"Great! When do I start?"

"Well, I guess just whenever you want to," I answered him.

"Uh," he hesitated. "I'll be needing a check. Where do I go to get my money?"

"To God." I studied him.

"Well, I'll see you later," he lamely offered. The conversation seemed to end his aspirations.

Another guy announced that he was called of God to travel the circuit and that he would need to move in the motor home with Ann and me for a while. I quickly discouraged that idea, all the while chuckling inside as I imagined Ann's reaction to an uninvited boarder.

But the situation we encountered at a national finals Rodeo in Oklahoma City was serious. The devil had very evidently masterminded a scheme to thwart, if not destroy, the beautiful work God had begun.

At the onset of the rodeo, as we began to outline the Christian activities, a young couple came to me. They announced that a man who had started a movement of which they were part was coming to town. They wanted him to speak to the cowboys and girls and were very, very insistent. It was an awkward position for me. I had never heard of the man or his organization. Yet, if I outrightly refused on those grounds, the cowboys and girls would think I was jealous of the ministry among them and unduly protective. Several of the young couple's friends were equally as adamant that the man be permitted to come. Having no real grounds upon which to refuse, I compromised, agreeing that one afternoon in the rodeo hotel, in a private room, the man could speak to all who wished to come.

After making that commitment, a great unrest came into my spirit. The uneasiness just would not disappear. I recollected that a friend of mine in Roswell, a businessman, had multiple ministry friends and contacts. Maybe he would recognize this man's name and be able to endorse his ministry. I called my friend and questioned him, giving the brief information about the minister that I had obtained from the couple. He said, "Glenn, this is strange. I know nothing about the man, but I am on another line to a man in California who researches and writes booklets on ministries in error, on counterfeit ministries. Let me ask him." He was gone a few moments and came back on the line. "Glenn." He sounded urgent. "This man has a highly deceptive ministry. It is a counterfeit of the abundant life in Jesus Christ. My California friend has just completed a booklet on him." He proceeded to quote me several things from the booklet as his friend was reading on the phone to him.

"This is a large and dangerous cult that preys primarily on younger people," the California man warned. "The cult leader's approach is one of intimidation, impressing you with his research and education. He bullies you into laying your reasoning aside and accepting his on the merit of his great intellectual prowess. He wants his followers to accept his interpretation of the Bible. He claims to have spent years alone with God and gotten special revelation that contradicts the Bible and that of solid Bible teachers."

I had a sinking feeling. What was I going to do now? If I confronted the man in the meeting, the young converts would not understand. They would see me in a bad light—probably believing me to be motivated by jealousy of the man's ministry. I prayed.

Feeling led of the Spirit to do so, I talked with Ron Conatser, Willard, and a couple of others who I felt would pray and stand with me. We bound the enemy, sought God's delivering power, and went to the meeting.

The room was lined with inquisitive faces when Dr. Deceiver arrived with his wife and a bodyguard or two. He sat, and without much preamble began to communicate his educational background and credentials. He threw in a couple of insights into the Scriptures, of which he bet we were unaware. The tactic of tearing down our confidence in our knowledge of the Bible and of establishing his more superior insight into the Scriptures was already at work. My California advisor was certainly correct so far. I was distressed and distraught. I could see the innocent faces in the room were drinking in his every word.

Suddenly, Ron stepped forward. He said, "Excuse me, sir. I would like to ask you to confess Jesus Christ as your Lord and Savior to this group, if you would."

"What?" The man's face was incredulous, then angry. "I've never been so insulted in all of my life," he spewed. "What right have you to ask me that?"

I had been sitting with my thumb on a certain passage of Scripture. When Ron interrupted, I knew it was time to read 1 John 4:1–3. I said, as I stood to my feet, "Perhaps this is where Ron gets his authority," and proceeded to read, "Beloved, believe not every spirit, but try the spirits whether they are of God: because many false prophets are gone out into the world. Hereby know ye the Spirit of God: Every spirit that confesseth that Jesus Christ is come in the flesh is of God: And every spirit that confesseth not that Jesus Christ is come in the flesh is not of God: and this is that spirit of antichrist, whereof ye have heard that it should come; and even now already is it in the world."

Ron persisted in asking for the man's confession of Jesus. As he became more angry and distraught, his wife came to his defense, stating things that didn't surprise me. My phone call had warned me of most of them. Finally, the frustrated man said, "Of course I can say that Jesus Christ is my Lord." However, he seemed unable to make a heart confession of Jesus as his personal Lord and again announced that he could never recall being so insulted. He hurled insults as he stood to leave. Opening the door to depart, he thrust one hand into his pocket and pulled out a package of cigarettes. About that time, a young believer, Jeff Coppenhaver, arrived at the door, intending to come to the meeting. Joyously filled with the Spirit, Jeff looked at the man, having no idea who he was, and noticed the cigarettes in his hand. "Jesus delivered me from those," Jeff exulted.

"I guess He delivered you from sex too," our departing guest speaker snapped as he fled the room.

It was easy to preach that Sunday. The anointing was so heavy it was almost visible. When I gave the invitation, many, many hands in the crowd, which far exceeded one thousand, went up. They then came forward to receive their Bibles and personal ministry. It was a glorious day in Oklahoma City.

At this same time, Ann and Karen Vold were able to set up a Christian women's brunch, getting in on the social calendar of the NFR activities. It quickly became a haven for hungry hearts, a welcome respite from the worldly activities, a place to receive strength and encouragement. Never has there been a shortage of testimonies, and through the simple invitation given at the close, many women have had the opportunity to receive Jesus in a personal way. It became an annual affair.

Chapter Eleven
GOD HAS THE LAST WORD

N 1979 I was talking and ministering to a cowboy in the rodeo arena at Odessa, Texas. Intent on our conversation, I did not see the one-eyed saddle bronc coming toward me until it was too late. He smashed me against the arena wall, breaking several ribs, puncturing my lungs, crushing my pelvis, and causing multiple other injuries, including internal bleeding.

The doctor's diagnosis and prognosis were terrible. I found myself in a hospital bed, undergoing severe pain and drugged to the point of unconsciousness.

Spirit-filled cowboys came to the hospital with their Bibles in their hands. They began to pray the Word of God over me and, along with Ann, believed that they received my healing. (I was mostly unconscious.) Speaking to the abnormal blood flow in my body, they commanded it be removed according to Mark 11:23. Next, they forbid the doctors to give me any more narcotics. When I was awake and able to make a choice, I chose to leave the hospital, trusting in the medicine of God's Word.

With the doctor and hospital staff protesting loudly, they placed me in a wheelchair and, in the midst of a blizzard, put me in the motor home. The doctors insisted that I must be in a cast for at least nine months and would probably not live if I left the hospital. Strangely, the moment I got outside the hospital and into the motor home the abnormal blood flow stopped, never to return. (Now, I do not recommend that others get up and leave a hospital because I did. Everyone must individually hear from God.)

Dennis McKinley drove my motor home through that terrible snowstorm to Denver, where a convention was going on. I lay on my bed in the convention hotel, and people would come to our room for ministry. Two weeks later I stood and preached at a rodeo in Texas, all because of the power in the Word of God.

Ministers' children are sometimes a special target of the enemy; ours were no exception. Being young, they did not always walk in the light of God's Word, and we spent many hours praying for them.

Calling Pam in Austin, we were chilled to hear of a diabolical attack on her life. Asleep one night in her apartment, she awoke to find a man attacking her. He had a knife at her throat. Although the pressure of the knife kept her from speaking loudly, she whispered, "In the name of Jesus and by His blood, get away from me." The man, startled, drew back his knife. Pam spoke loudly, "Get out of here in the name of Jesus."

The evil spirit controlling the man screamed, "Don't say that name!"

Pam yelled, "The name of Jesus, the name of Jesus! Get out in the name of Jesus!"

The man shuddered with fear, screamed loudly, and ran out of her apartment. Seeing the visible effect of

Jesus' name and more confident in her authority than ever, Pam actually chased the man down the street, screaming, "The name of Jesus," as he fled. Needless to say, we praised God for her deliverance.

Some time before we went on the road full-time as a family, Ann and I had felt impressed to receive by faith an airplane. Since then, we had occasionally praised the Lord for the plane, believing it would come in His timing.

By 1979, we were more intensely praising Him for its manifestation because the need was evident. Calls from all over the country were coming, asking us to hold Sunday, sometimes Saturday, services at smaller rodeos in areas where no commercial airport existed. We traveled so continually on the ground that it was virtually impossible to extend ourselves much further. Therefore, we could not accept many of the invitations we felt we should. A plane would solve our problem.

Driving past the Lubbock, Texas, airport one day in June, I felt the urge to pull in and go inside. There, pinned on the bulletin board, was a picture of the very type of plane for which I was believing. It was for sale.

I found the sales manager and asked him about the plane. He told me it was temporarily in San Angelo. A veterinarian was flying it while his plane was being repaired. The manager offered to fly us over to look at the plane. A few days later, we accepted his offer. He flew to Roswell, picked us up, and took us to San Angelo.

It was a case of love at first sight. I knew that I knew that I knew that we had found our plane. A Cessna 206, loaded with the finest equipment, turbo charged, it was painted a patriotic red, white, and blue. It was a beauty. Ann and I laid hands on it, received it into the ministry, and told the salesman, "Yes, this is the plane we want." We told him that we did not know exactly how the Lord intended to handle the financial end of the matter, but that He would. (At this point, we had the sum of two hundred dollars in our plane account.) We took a couple of pictures of the plane and returned home.

I put a picture of the plane in my pocket and one on the motor home mirror. Ann and I praised God for our plane, confessed we had it, and by physical sight nothing was happening. I wanted that plane in our possession so badly that I got downright miserable, and my natural reasoning took over. I went to the bank. They agreed to finance the plane—no problem at all. As I went home to tell Ann of the bank's approval of the loan, I knew in my heart that it was not God's perfect will for us to borrow for the plane. One look at her face confirmed the feeling in my heart. She said gently, "Glenn, this is not God's best in this. It is not His perfect way or will." Knowing she was right, I dropped the matter. When the man would call and ask if we had the money for the plane, saying he needed to know because another party was interested, I would tell him to go ahead and show it to anyone he pleased, but that the plane was mine, and God would make the way.

That is how it stood when we left Roswell and drove to Albuquerque for the rodeo and our services there. Preacher and Arlene Stevens from Oklahoma were there a little early also, and we visited and fellowshiped together. They were believing with us for our plane. In fact, they were the people God used to put the two hundred dollars in our airplane account.

The next day I prepared to go to the airport to pick up John Copeland, Kenneth and Gloria Copeland's son. He was coming to Albuquerque to spend a few days with us during the rodeo. In his mid-teens, John was a good-looking youngster and certainly all boy. The professional cowboys took right to John, and vice versa. I could always find him during the bull riding for sure. He would be back behind the chutes. Once, during the San Antonio rodeo, to my horror, I found him in the pen with the bulls.

Ambling off the plane, John saw me and grinned. I hugged him, and we finally made it to the car. Once inside, John handed me an envelope and related, "Daddy said for me to give you this as soon as I got here." I took the envelope and stuffed it into the glove compartment, thinking it contained parental instructions regarding John's school assignments. John watched me and said, "No, Glenn. Daddy said for you to open it when I got here." He took it out of the glove compartment and handed it to me as I was approaching the cashier's booth to pay out of the airport parking lot.

There was a car in front of us, and as we waited, I opened the envelope. Inside was a handwritten note from Kenneth: "Dear Glenn, please agree with me for the finances at Eagle Mountain. Go get your plane. We love you, Ken." Folded inside the note was a check for the entire balance of the plane. I was beside myself. I didn't notice that the car in front of me had moved, and I began to shout, cry, laugh, and praise God all at the same time. John sat beside me laughing, looking quite pleased with himself.

Finally, I gained control of myself, and I returned to the rodeo grounds. There, Ann and I rejoiced together, and Preacher and Arlene Stevens joined us in praising God. I hardly slept that night, I was so elated. It was the next day, I believe, before I could get Kenneth and Gloria on the phone to thank them. It was hard to find words to convey to them the gratitude I felt for their unselfish love.

Brother Ken's letter hangs framed on my office wall as a constant reminder of God's faithfulness. I pray for Brother Ken and Gloria and their ministry every time I look at it.

Chapter Twelve

ENLARGE THE PLACE
OF THY TENT

THROUGH CONTACTS MADE through professional rodeo, doors opened to establish services at various junior and high school rodeos throughout the country. Dennis and I flew to Yakima, Washington, to conduct a service at the National High School Rodeo Finals. To my knowledge, it was the first of its kind. Hundreds of young people and their parents attended, sitting in the stands. More than one hundred of the contestants sat horseback, row after row, intently listening to the gospel, many for the first time. A great many of them committed their lives and hearts to the Lord Jesus—so many that we ran out of Bibles and literature. Later, Dennis and I conducted a baptismal service at a local motel swimming pool.

Invited to preach at the American Junior Rodeo Association Finals in Snyder, Texas, we were thrilled. We asked Paul and Gail Petska from Carlsbad, New Mexico, to go with us. Gail was a former (several times) world champion barrel racer, and Paul an outstanding roper, who, with his brother Monty, became an NFR team roping finalist more times than one. They were respected by others in professional rodeo, and God used them mightily. We planned to take the plane, pick them up in Carlsbad, and all fly over together. The service was set for 2 P.M. on a Tuesday.

Excited over the opportunity to reach the western-minded youth, as well as their parents, we eagerly anticipated the service. Tuesday arrived, along with totally instrument-flying weather. It was apparent my VFR license would be of no benefit in the cloudy overhang. I contacted an instrument-rated pilot, who, in spite of such short notice, agreed to fly us in my plane to Snyder via Carlsbad to pick up the Petskas.

After a short stop in Carlsbad, the Petskas aboard, we took off in dreadful looking weather. In the middle of a heavy rainstorm, air traffic control contacted us and told us to change our course. Reaching down between the two front seats to retrieve his map to plot the new course, our pilot experienced vertigo.

Sitting in the right front seat, it took me a few moments to realize what was happening. Glancing at the plane instruments, I knew immediately that we were in a graveyard spiral to the right. I immediately started recovery procedures, reducing the throttle, leveling the wings. As all of this transpired, our instrument pilot sat as if paralyzed, in a state of vertigo, until the wings were leveled, and we broke out of the clouds some fifteen hundred feet above ground. I praised God both for His delivering power and for the fact that our backseat passengers seemed unaware of their close scrape with death and of the cockpit drama.

Awaiting us in Snyder were Kent and Sharon Youngblood. Kent is a past president of the Cowboy

Chapter of the FCA. Awarded the Rookie of the Year honor his first year as a PRCA calf roper, Kent is an irrepressible practical joker and serious only, it sometimes seems, in regard to his relationship with the Lord. His very quiet and ladylike wife, Sharon, is one of rodeo's outstanding barrel racers and trainers. They have long been friends and partners of this ministry.

I was overwhelmed with the turnout. The room in the coliseum was packed with young folks and their families. And as the Holy Spirit fell on that place, their eyes, young and old, were riveted on the singers, those testifying (Paul and Gail did a bang up job), and me as I preached. I was careful to keep it simple and to present as clearly as possible God's availability to man through Jesus Christ.

Giving the invitation, I was absolutely astounded at the response. A host of young people and parents raised their hands to receive the Lord, then swarmed forward to receive Bibles, other literature, and prayer. It was tremendous!

A rancher by the name of Tom Figg had contacted me while we were in Austin, Texas, and invited me to come to Montana to preach at a high school district rodeo. Watching our cat, Jennifer, bounce across the dash of our motor home as Ann and I traveled at the cautious speed of about twenty-five miles per hour down a very rough dirt road on our way to Ekalaka, Montana, I wondered what had possessed me. How far had I missed God? We surveyed the empty landscape with interest (at that pace we had time to inspect most of it) and were persuaded that this mission qualified as the "uttermost parts of the earth."

Finally arriving in the unique little town of Ekalaka in our dust-caked vehicle, I contacted Tom. So shy that he only occasionally glanced at my face as he talked, the nice-looking young rancher outlined plans for the rodeo service the next day. Tom had been saved for a while, and it suddenly occurred to him that he needed to do something to reach others in his area with the Word of the Lord. He had heard of me through the Cowboy Chapter, FCA.

The next morning we drove to the rodeo grounds in Ekalaka and set up my portable pulpit and waited. A local minister's wife was providing the music from the arena floor on her electric piano. To my amazement, the stands we were using soon filled. After a few local specials I stood and preached a simple four-point sermon and gave the invitation. Again, the response was startling. Not only did many of the youth receive Jesus, but also men who had ranched and farmed in that rural area responded in a very dramatic way. It was as though the Spirit of God chose that little rodeo service to begin to touch and to change the complexion of the entire town. Through subsequent visits and ministry, we could see that is exactly what He did.

As we sat on the rodeo grounds in the afternoon, person after person came for ministry—from bank employees to ranchers and farmers. Someone came to me and asked if I would preach at the Congregational Church of Christ that evening. I said I would.

Parked in the front of the church late in the evening, we still had one fellow in the motor home who had been there interminably, it seemed, asking question after question. A rancher, Erlend Laird, wanted to know how to get God in on every aspect of his business. He was particularly interested in God's principles in the area of giving and receiving. He wanted out of debt and knew he had to do it God's way. I spent so much time with Erlend that I had to time to prepare for the service that night. In fact, he was still there when I excused myself to change clothes. I had no idea at all what I was to share with these people. I uttered a short prayer, "Father, if anything gets done here tonight, it will certainly have to be You. I trust You to get Your will done through me, for I yield to Your Spirit in Jesus' name."

I think everyone was shocked at the size of the crowd in the little Congregational church that night. The building was packed. The pastor was more than gracious, and after a few songs turned the service over to me.

It is very difficult to describe what happened from that point. I actually remember only standing up to preach. The Spirit of God fell in that little church so powerfully that my watch stopped, and the taping equipment (more than one set) failed to operate. I felt caught up in a vacuum, totally enveloped to God's Spirit. I opened my mouth, and out came a torrent. Ann and others later told me that I preached the gospel from beginning to end, emphasizing the present-day ministry of Jesus Christ, who is the same yesterday, today, and forever. I imparted God's yearning to heal the sick and the need for the baptism in the Spirit of God to carry out the ministry of Jesus today.

Nobody moved. It seemed they hardly breathed. It was as though the Holy Spirit reached into every person and gripped them by the reins of their heart and said, "Listen up. I have something to say to you. It is time to quit playing church and demonstrate Jesus."

When I quit speaking, my knees buckled, and I sank down on the first pew. No one moved for a long while. Eventually the little pastor arose and came to the front and stood there shaking his head, as though to bring himself to. He finally said, "What can I say? God has spoken to us tonight." It was an awesome occasion, to say the least.

This was only the first of many trips to Ekalaka. A Spirit-filled church body sprang up, and God sent a pastor. People all over that Montana area received Jesus as Lord and the baptism in His Spirit and began to share Him far and wide. Through faithful folks in the Ekalaka area, God began to establish a small crew of partners who faithfully supported this ministry financially and prayerfully. For a couple of years, our ministry went down the road primarily on offerings and tithes coming out of that tiny ranching area.

Aside from the numerous junior and high school rodeos to which we began to send others, we continued to pioneer works at other rodeos, including services at the Indian National Finals Rodeo in Albuquerque, New Mexico. There I bravely preached on cowboys and Indians and God's love for both, seeing about seventy people receive the Lord. It was thrilling to me—I am part Sioux—to preach to the Indian Nation with almost every Indian tribe represented and to observe a real breakthrough by the Spirit of God. Those Indian folks are dear to us, and we have had opportunity to preach to them under circumstances other than the rodeo. Invited to a campmeeting (in the truest sense of the word), Ann and I drove our motor home to the top of a mountain outside of Lodgegrass, Montana, where we ministered to the Cheyenne and Crow Nations for three days, seeing many receive Jesus and other special miracles and healings.

We traveled the west coast, establishing services at some of the rodeos out there. California seemed a brand new western mission field with its own brand of cowboys and girls who eagerly embraced the gospel.

In Santa Monica, California, Ann and I had just gone to bed when we heard a knock on the motor home door. Opening it, I saw a barrel racer holding the bridle to her horse, which was in a real mess. Blood was streaming from his nostrils, and as he slung his head, trying to breathe, blood was splattering the outsides of the motor home. She begged me to pray. Reaching inside the motor home, I grasped my Bible. Feeling led of the Spirit to pray Ezekiel 16:6 for the horse, I did so. It says, in part, "I said unto thee when thou wast in thy blood, Live." I commanded the horse to be healed in Jesus' name.

To the barrel racer's great joy (and my relief), the blood stopped flowing immediately. The horse was healed, and she was soon riding it in the arena. It didn't take long for that testimony to spread.

After our tour of the west coast, Dennis McKinley began to cover that area as the ministry continued there, growing by leaps and bounds.

CAMPMEETINGS

Paul and Gail Petska, Willard Moody, Barry and Cheryl Burk, and some of the other cowboys and girls wanted to have a cowboy campmeeting in Carlsbad after Christmas before the rodeo season started. I invited Tommy Williams to speak along with me, and he accepted. We took an extra motor home down for Tommy and Jo Ann, and all of us parked at the Petskas' place. We used a nearby gymnasium for our meetings. The power of God fell as we worshiped, taught, preached, and ministered to a hungry group of young Christians.

It was a memorable occasion for another reason also: Rev. Coy Huffman and his wife, Donna, entered the rodeo scene and our lives at this point. I can't recall how they knew of the meeting at Carlsbad, but they were there. Graduated from a Bible school in Washington State and having ministered in the Philippines and elsewhere, Coy and Donna were especially interested in the cowboy world. Coy had rodeoed both as an amateur and a professional, much as I had, and once a cowboy, always a cowboy.

I invited Coy to preach at one of the sessions, and I could see at once that he was a man of the Word and an able minister. Coy and Donna went with us over to Odessa, Texas, the first rodeo of the year, and a few after that. All the while, they were seeking God in regard to the exact spot He had for them. It wasn't long before He showed them: Canada. They were called to pioneer a work in the Canadian rodeos, much as Ann and I had in the United States.

Once they were sure they had heard from God, Coy and Donna were off to Canada, where they proved their apostolic calling in a tremendous way with exciting results.

After some years of concentrating on Canada, Coy and Donna returned to the United States' rodeo scene, originating many services where we were not going, and as the Lord led Ann and me to pull off of some of the places we had pioneered, I relinquished them to Coy with great confidence. His ministry is one of integrity. For a while, Coy and Donna operated under this ministry along with Larry Smith and Dennis McKinley.

Now that we were no longer alone in ministry on the rodeo circuit, now that God had sent and raised up such able ministers, we felt free to spend more time off the circuit in other types of meetings. Under the leadership of the Holy Spirit, we began to set up cowboy campmeetings in ranch and farm areas.

One of the first was in Iraan, Texas, at the ranch of the McMullan clan—not only Kenny and Glenda but also their family. In fact, we had a built-in audience with the McMullans alone! We began to meet in their barn in November of each year. Some of the finest meetings imaginable have taken place in that barn filled with area ranchers and country folks (and a few people from town). Souls have found Jesus, bodies have been healed, and a multiplicity of other Holy Spirit events have taken place. Bedrock partners of this ministry have come from this area.

Aside from holding Sunday grandstand services at the Spooner Rodeo in Spooner, Wisconsin, I began, as the Holy Spirit gave contacts, to hold meetings in Bloomer and Spooner. Dairy farmer Denny Huse, along with his wife, Gail, began to set up our meetings in that area. We began to see miracles of salvation as that hungry crew gathered to hear God's Word. A Holy Spirit explosion began to occur among the Huses' family and friends. Again, God added partners to this ministry.

Perhaps one of the warmest and most enjoyable yearly campmeetings that we have done has been at Summerville, Georgia. (Home of Charlie and Wanda Lowry, our meetings are ordinarily in the sleepy little community of Gore, a little way out of Summerville.) Charlie, whose southern drawl outdoes any I've ever heard, is a champion roper and steer wrestler, having won all sorts of titles. One year at Cheyenne, when he won the title of All-Around Cowboy, he received the buckle every cowboy covets. Cheyenne is special. Charlie took off the big buckle he had been wearing, which he had won elsewhere, and gave it to me as he clipped the Cheyenne prize on his belt. I've been wearing Charlie's buckle ever since. Weighing less than one hundred and fifty pounds, I hardly look as though I could have won the big steer wrestling buckle, but I refuse to let that intimidate me.

The amusing thing to me about our meetings in the Lowrys' area is that every year most or many of those attending our campmeeting are school teachers. Of course, Wanda is a teacher, and that probably accounts for why so many of them attend. One time a translator in Mexico City told the people to excuse him when I was preaching. He said he had to translate from cowboy to English and then to Spanish. When I look at all those teachers Ann and I have come to love so much, I think, "God is truly using the foolish to confound the wise."

Fort Davis, Texas, is probably our favorite spot on earth. We happened onto Fort Davis when the mother of a high school rodeo champion asked us there to hold a meeting. There was only a handful of people in the gymnasium that night, but God began a work, which He continued.

The next day, James and Jan Dyer, who attended the meeting, invited us out to their ranch nestled in all those knobby hills. It is a breathtakingly beautiful location. We experienced an immediate rapport with them and with their family, who also lives in that area.

Fort Davis itself is an intrigue to many visitors. It sits en route to Big Bend National Park and boasts quaint and unique buildings. The drugstore has not progressed in service and atmosphere past the fifties. You can actually order a soda-fountain cherry or vanilla Coke or old-fashioned soda.

After returning to Fort Davis a few times to minister in various and sundry places, including the Dyers' home and the Catholic parish hall, we felt strongly impressed of the Lord to begin a yearly believer's convention and to locate it at the picturesque Prude Ranch, both a dude and actual working ranch in the hills outside Fort Davis.

We secured the Prude Ranch facilities, invited guest speakers and singers, and printed brochures, mailing them to our friends and partners. We awaited the meeting prayerfully and hopefully. We had never put our necks on the line quite so thoroughly, but we believed the meetings were of God and fervently reminded ourselves of that fact.

Sure enough, before the first Friday meeting, campers, motor homes, and cars steadily trickled onto the grounds. By Saturday we had a crowd that well exceeded our expectations, and we praised God. The meetings, held in a huge gymnasium, went tremendously well. A family atmosphere prevailed with so many of our friends and partners present. That Memorial Day weekend convention was to be the first of many.

In March of one year, I drove to Fort Davis to check on details pertaining to our upcoming convention in May. Ann had flown to the West Coast to an intercessors convention. I was tired, bone tired, and more uptight than I could or would admit. I checked with Prude Ranch and spent the night with James and Jan Dyer. Before I left, they watched me strangely and insisted on praying for me. I thanked them and left for home, feeling almost as bleak as the sky, which was beginning to fill with large flakes of snow.

I had not driven many miles on that lonely road when I felt like my blood had begun to boil. Suddenly I experienced a crushing in my chest and a feeling that something had exploded inside me. All strength left me. My arms and hands became numb. I barely managed to pull off the road. I looked at my fingernails. They were turning blue. I opened my mouth in an attempt to pray but could not speak. I finally was able to get the window down a slight bit by pushing the button. I leaned my head against the window, gasping for air as snowflakes drifted in on my forehead. The thought came, "I've bought the farm." I weakly brushed that thought aside. "Jesus, help me." I could only think the words.

I was lifelessly watching the phone posts, fence, and trees outside my window. Suddenly, it seemed they came alive. The words came to me loud and clear, actually entering my body and giving it strength: "Because I live, you shall live also." That is all it took—seven words from Jesus. It was as though all of creation echoed those words as they brought life to me. Strengthened by the Word of God Himself, I was able to drive the distance back to Roswell and to continue on schedule as usual.

Later I learned that the friend who was with Ann at the intercessors convention had dropped to her knees at the very moment I was struck with the heart attack and began to pray for me. (They had noticed the time, and so had I.) Also, I received a letter from an Australian friend who had been impressed to pray for me at that exact time. How I praise God for His praying children!

Chapter Thirteen
MANIFESTATIONS
OF THE WORD

WE PIONEERED QUITE a few areas with campmeetings, returning time after time to many of the same parts of the country. Churches began to form out of some of the meetings, and after a time God supernaturally sent pastors to shepherd His flock.

One day I was over at Pastor Alan Grainger's church in Las Cruces, New Mexico. Brother Lester Sumrall was there, and Alan had a special get-together for other ministers to meet and learn from Dr. Sumrall. He asked each of us to state our ministry calling. Most of the men present were pastors, with maybe a field ministry or two. When he got to me, I said, "I am an apostle and an evangelist."

He snorted and said abruptly, "Don't tell anyone you are an apostle."

Before I could say anything else he went on to the next person. I was embarrassed and a little bit put out with him. All I had done to the best of my knowledge was tell him what he had asked.

Later at the fellowship, I went up to Dr. Sumrall and asked, "Sir, I'd like you to tell me why I should not have told you I was an apostle. I do very similar things to what you have done, and you call yourself an apostle."

Dr. Sumrall said, "Sit down." I sat. He asked, "Do you have churches spring out of your work?" I said I did. "Do you go into foreign countries?" I assured him I did. He asked other questions—such as, Do I go into areas where no other ministry has gone?—and all my answers were affirmative. He sat back and admitted, "You are an apostle. I was wrong."

God had led Ann to what is now our home in Roswell in a very supernatural way. She had desired a spot where she could see out. Having been raised in the rolling ranchland area of the Panhandle of Texas, she felt crowded in the townhouse we were leasing. Real estate people seemed unable to help. Nothing seemed appropriate for us personally or for our rapidly expanding ministry headquarters. We were being forced to move. The townhouse had sold, and we were up against a real deadline.

Flying back from San Antonio to take our newsletter copy to the printer in Roswell, Ann felt impressed that the Lord was going to show her the location of our house. After going to the printer she asked Jay to drive out west of town. As they passed a dirt road six miles out of town, Ann saw a house with a rock fireplace. She said, "That is like where I would like to live." After looking elsewhere to no avail, Ann said, "Jay, drive up there, and let's look at the house I saw on the top of the hill. Maybe something up there is for sale."

As they drove up to the house, they could see a For Sale sign on the front of the property. Ann was overjoyed,

especially when she and Jay looked into the many win-
dows and saw that it was just perfect for our home and
for temporary ministry headquarters. Calling the realtor,
Ann found that the house had just been dropped in price
by twenty thousand dollars! She called me, glowingly
describing her find, and I encouraged her to make an offer
on it. She did so, and the Lord did "exceedingly abun-
dantly more than we could ask or think," giving us great
favor with the seller. The owner was willing to work with
us on the equity, giving us several months to pay it completely. (The Lord saw to it that we paid it much sooner
than we were required.)

Within a few short days we were the proud owners
of a house that was surely the answer to many fervent
prayers. Out of our kitchen window we view the often
snow-covered mountain range at Ruidoso, and out of the
front, at night, we especially enjoyed the twinkling lights
of Roswell below.

Lock, stock, and baggage, we moved both ministry
and personal items into the house. The property was
nearly three acres in an oblong strip that provided a complete empty lot facing a back road. We knew that our
office would sit on that property. We just didn't know
how. But we knew that God knew, and we began immediately to trust Him to manifest an office back there for
us. We received it in prayer and began to thank God
that it was there. By the eye of faith, we could see it. We
began to call our office into being by faith, just as "God,
who quickeneth the dead, and calleth those things which
be not as though they were" (Rom. 4:17).

When visitors were at our house I might say, as we looked out toward the mountains past our property, "Do you see that office building there behind us?" When they looked at me blankly, I would assure them that it was there. It was real to Ann, Jay, and me. We believed we had received it, and we knew it would show up. God would somehow cause it to do so.

One day a man named Jack Swanson showed up at our house. Jack had begun to come to our motor home years before, and at the rodeo at San Angelo, which is his home town, he had prayed to receive Jesus as his Lord. Jack, his wife, Mary Lou, and their children had become true friends and partners of our in the ministry. Jack drove up and pulled out two sets of plans. He announced that he had taken the liberty to have them drawn up for an office. He made some suggestions, and we settled on the plans.

A short time later, Jack and Mary Lou were back with their sons and employees. After preparing the ground, they poured the slab for our office. They were soon back to frame and roof it. Jack, a genius at finding bargains, sent our roof from a place in Texas! Thank God for godly businessmen who heed the voice of the Holy Spirit. Stage by stage our office progressed.

At one point we were out of funds to invest in it. We needed about ten thousand dollars to continue. During this period, Ann and I were at the National Finals Rodeo in Oklahoma City. The local chapter of the FCA sponsored, for several years, a luncheon for the Christian cowboys and others. We always attended and were waiting in line to enter the banquet room.

A man I had only met a time or two, Mark Woods, walked up to me and put a check in my hand. I thanked him and prayed a blessing back to him in faith. I stood there, joking with Willard Moody, and handed him the check. He opened it and looked amazed. He said, "I'd be happy with the tithe off this check, Glenn," as he handed it back to me. I looked at the check in astonishment. It was for ten thousand dollars—just what we needed to continue our work on the office!

Dennis, Richard Ashley, and Jay completed the inside of the office, and I painted and hung maps and paper. At last our office was a reality! We dedicated it to the Lord, praising Him for His faithfulness and also for the obedience of those whom He had used to provide it. Jay was especially thrilled to have his own apartment, which was constructed on the end of the office in order that someone be on the ministry premises at all times.

Now that God had established our first office in Roswell, New Mexico, one day we arrived at our office out on Six-mile Hill and found ourselves locked out. Jay had changed the locks in our absence for necessary reasons. I was tired and down-hearted; I was hungry and had hoped to get at least twenty dollars from the cash box in the office so we might go out to eat. (We were out of cash and used no credit cards in those days.) Jay was nowhere to be found.

I began to talk to the heavenly Father saying, "Father, all I needed was twenty dollars. Ann and I are hungry, and we're tired. You know we have been out on the road non-stop ministering Your Word and winning souls to Jesus. It just doesn't seem right." I was actually having a pity party and crying on the Father's shoulder.

Suddenly a tumbleweed blew up to my boot tip and stopped. It had a twenty dollar bill stuck in the middle of it! I had trouble believing my eyes. As I took it out I began to laugh and cry and thank the Lord. It was as though God said, "I'm the same Father who put the coin in the fish's month" (Matt. 17:27). Just think of God's amazing timing and perfect orchestration of such an event. How very awesome is our Lord!

VEHICLES

Ann had been believing God for a larger car once we were established in more permanent ministry headquarters. In fact, she had asked for a Cadillac. It wasn't long until she was driving a beautiful white El Dorado, courtesy of the Lord.

She had been driving it only a few months when she began to have thoughts out of nowhere about our pastor's wife driving the car. When she would go out to get in the car she would think, "This is Sandy Brown's car." Strongly suspecting that these were the Lord's thoughts and not her own, she finally prayed, "Lord, if You want us to give this car to Mike and Sandy, let Glenn know, and I am willing."

A few days later we were sitting in Denny's Restaurant drinking coffee. I looked at Ann and said, "I don't know how you are going to handle this, but the Lord just spoke to me and told me we were to give your car to Mike and Sandy Brown."

She didn't bat an eye. Instead, she urged, "Let's do it now. It's the Lord. He told me the same thing." We went home, and I took the car to wash and clean it up.

When it was as spotless as we could get it, we drove it over to the Browns' house and gave it to them. They were both incredulous and overjoyed. Their car had collapsed, mainly because of age and miles, and they had been asking God what they were to do. We thanked God for permitting us to be in on fulfilling a need in another part of His body, and began to believe Him to cause His laws of sowing and reaping to work on our behalf in regard to vehicles.

Before long we were driving an even newer and nicer car, but God wasn't through channeling vehicles through us to others (especially ministries). When we began to get comfortable or a little attached to a car or truck, the Holy Spirit would instruct us concerning its next owner, and we endeavored to obey. I did argue with Him a bit about a white Mustang I was especially fond of but finally gave in, knowing my Father knows best. We continued to trust Him to meet our needs in various areas of transportation.

We felt that we needed a more adequate means of transporting tapes, Bibles, and other ministry supplies to various campmeetings and had begun to believe God for a truck that would do the job. One summer I was at a Kenneth Copeland seminar, and he had invited Hilton

Sutton as a guest speaker. Hilton had brought a lot of tapes, books, and materials with him, and the truck that was carrying his supplies was pulled into the coliseum to unload. I walked over to look at it. It was exactly the size and type our ministry needed. I asked some questions about it and visited with Hilton for a few minutes. I had never personally met him, although we appreciated his ministry.

A few weeks later I was home when the phone rang. It was Hilton. He informed me that he felt instructed by the Holy Spirit to give his truck to our ministry. He needed a bigger truck, a semi, and wanted to sow his smaller one and believe for his scriptural return. Hilton was rejoicing in God's methods and goodness and seemed absolutely thrilled to be able to obey the Lord in helping us. I was equally as thrilled and thanked him profusely. Hilton asked if he could use the truck to complete the run of meetings he was on before returning to his office. I assured him that was fine with me. A while later, Jay flew to Houston and received the truck from Hilton's staff and drove it proudly home.

A few years later, we needed a large amount of money to be totally free of debt on a motor home we had purchased several months earlier. We regularly praised God for supplying the sum needed, thus lifting a rather heavy financial burden off of us. We reminded Him that we had obeyed His command to give and knew that it would be given to us just as He had promised. December rolled around. By physical sight our financial situation did not look too encouraging. Yet, we knew that God is faithful.

On December 31, I went to the post office. In our box was a slip of paper telling me to claim a larger article at the window. At first I thought it was only some unclaimed newsletters being returned to us and didn't bother to pick up whatever it was. Thinking about it later, I decided to go back to the post office and see what was there. The postal clerk brought out a huge registered express mail envelope. In it was a small brown envelope—one of our partner envelopes. I opened it, and I almost fainted. In it was a check for twenty-five thousand dollars and a note: "Go pay off your motor home."

I rushed home to show the check to Ann and Jay. How we rejoiced and praised God for His provision and His timing! Then, I went to the bank and paid off the motor home. We were able to start the new year free of financial concern.

ANGELS

I was preaching in Bismarck, North Dakota, at the invitation of Trish Lenihan. On Sunday I was to preach at a match roping between two champion cowboys. It was all very awkward. They had it planned for me to climb up in the announcer's box to preach over the sound system. Being up there separated me so far from the people that it seemed I was preaching to empty air. Down below me around the arena, I could see people milling around, doing their thing, as I attempted to present a very simple and short sermon on God's love. I stressed the necessity of being born again and asked that anyone desiring to receive

Jesus come talk to me as soon as I dismounted the speaker's stand.

I climbed down, feeling a bit discouraged, and began to walk down the side of the arena. Walking with my head down and hat on, I came to a halt when I saw two sets of feet planted in front of mine. Looking up, I gazed into the most remarkable pair of eyes I've ever seen. They seemed to literally go through me. They were filled with compassion, love, and wisdom beyond this world. The man possessing those eyes did not fit out there amid western boots and hats. He was perfectly groomed, wearing a flawlessly tailored, and obviously expensive, silver-gray suit, shiny black shoes, and was topped with a silvery-white head of hair that is impossible to accurately describe. He was perfectly built.

He looked at me, pointed, and said, "This man would like to receive Jesus." As he looked in my eyes and said that, my knees wobbled, and several unconfessed sins (ones I must have considered minor) came to my mind. I felt dirty and sinful. Trying to get a grip on myself, I turned to look at his partner, the one he said needed to receive Jesus. My eyes traveled upward—nearly seven feet upward—to view one of the tallest black men I've ever seen.

I asked him, "Did you understand what I said about needing to ask Jesus into your heart?" When he answered in the affirmative, I asked that they bow their heads, and I led the man in a brief prayer to receive Jesus.

After saying, "Amen," I looked up. The silvery-haired man, the one who had convicted me of my sins, was nowhere to be seen. I looked at the ground, which was covered with powdery dust. I could see where both sets of footprints of the men had walked up to me. I could see the prints where the man who had brought the black man had stood in front of me. But there were no prints where he had walked away. Flustered beyond description, I asked the tall black man, "Where did your friend go?"

Answering in an accent I knew was not American, he replied, "What friend?"

I said, in near exasperation, "The man who brought you over here to me!"

He answered, "I don't know. I don't know where he went. I was sitting listening to you, and when you began to tell us that we needed Jesus in our hearts, that man came and sat by me. When you finished, he said to me, 'You need to receive Jesus. Come with me.' I followed him, and he led me to you. That is all I know about him."

As I stood pondering the set of footprints that ended there in front of me beside the tall black fellow, I knew why I had felt sinful and dirty. I knew why those eyes went all the way through me and why my knees had buckled. I had been in the presence of an angel of God; there was no other explanation.

The rest of the miracle was yet to unfold. Visiting with the black man, I found that he had just arrived in America from Ethiopia, had just happened to attend our little roping. With that beautiful accent, he said, "Now I must go tell my people about Jesus." It dawned on me that the evangelist Philip had little on me. In fact, we had a great deal in common.

The Ethiopian convert came to our meeting in town

that night. A special offering was taken for him to assist him on his way. Standing before the congregation with the bucket of cash in his arms, he smiled broadly. "God gave to me. Now, I give back to God." He grabbed handfuls of bills and shoved them into the hands of the ministers in charge of the meeting. Just newly born in the kingdom, with no teaching on giving and receiving, the Ethiopian somehow knew he was to share his blessings with others, beginning his Christian walk in the most selfless way possible.

There was another angelic happening. I was preaching in a part of Texas where there is a great deal of oppression. The Lord had instructed me to preach on spiritual warfare. Yet, the group who had invited me seemed actually afraid of the subject. I decided to obey God. I could feel a powerful anointing as I preached that day. You could see that the Spirit of God was getting His message through to the people.

After the service a lady came to me and told me that she had visibly seen an angel behind me as I preached, following me step by step, everywhere I went. In a few minutes, a man walked up to me and told me the very same thing!

Chapter Fourteen
AUSTRALIA, GOD LOVES YOU!

I COULDN'T SAY THAT I had always known that I would one day go to Australia, so it was quite unexpected when in late fall of 1981, Australia and its huge western world was on my mind. I couldn't figure out why until I saw something called the World Cup Rodeo advertised in the Professional Rodeo Cowboys Association *Sports News*. The rodeo was to begin right after Christmas and run into January of the coming year. It was advertised as the ultimate in rodeo, with a tremendous amount of money at stake. Obviously, American and Canadian cowboys would be flying there to compete. The Holy Spirit deeply impressed me that He intended to begin a work Down Under that would be similar to His move among cowboys in the United States.

I made plane reservations for two, and we began to trust the Lord for the funds to make the very expensive trip. In a couple of weeks, we were in Tulsa attending a meeting. Our friends and partners, Erlend and Thealou Laird, flew down from Ekalaka, Montana, to visit with us as well as to attend the seminar. We were visiting in our motor home, and I shared with them the need to stand with us for the Australian trip. They could see that it was of God and were excited.

We went on to the meeting and sat down by a

minister and his wife whom we knew. When the offering was taken, I felt led to give a check to the minister instead of to the regular meeting offering.

Ann and I started down the aisle at the close of the meeting, making our way out of the meeting hall. A pastor from Montana stopped me and told me the Lord had impressed him to send a certain amount of money for our trip to Australia. We were thrilled.

A little while later, we were back in our motor home with the Lairds, and Erland took out his checkbook and wrote a check and handed it to me. It exactly made up the balance of what we needed for two to make the trip to Australia! We praised God, knowing that our upcoming trip was undeniably of Him.

Back at home, Ann began to have the sneaking suspicion that she was not to go with me on this first junket Down Under. Committing herself to prayer, she heard the will of God. He told her that Dennis McKinley was to take her ticket and to go with me, that God needed Dennis down there also. She gritted her spiritual teeth and told me what the Lord had said. I hated for her to stay behind but could see how Dennis would be a tremendous witness and minister to those guys on the opposite side of the world and, so, agreed that Dennis could go in her place. Come to find out, Dennis knew he was to go and had really been praying. He was overjoyed to hear the news that his prayers were answered. He was on his way to Australia.

The day after Christmas, Dennis, Kent Youngblood, a host of American cowboy contestants, and I began the very long and tiring trip. Landing eventually in Melbourne, where the rodeo would begin, we were excited and filled with expectation.

God gave us great favor with the Australian press and all those in authority. We were quickly able to find a building on the fair and rodeo grounds in which to hold meetings each day after each rodeo. We had only a handful in the congregation the first day. But word traveled quickly, and the next day the attendance doubled—and continued to do so each day. God began to do exactly as He had in our early years on the United States' rodeo circuit. By the power of His Spirit, He drew the names in Australian rodeo, saving and healing the "toughs" and healing horses to gain the attention of some of the contestants. Ali Smith, a Miss Rodeo Australia who had recently given her life to the Lord, brought her barrel racing horse for prayer. He couldn't see out his right eye. The Lord supernaturally touched the horse, and Ali won the next go-round. That miracle got our meetings a lot of attention.

The third day, Ali's fiancé, Graham Heffernan, came to the meeting and gave his life to Jesus. Graham, one of Australia's outstanding rodeo champions, made a tremendous impact on the other contestants.

These initial meetings in Australia were dramatically Holy Spirit-led and blessed get-togethers. It was very, very evident God had zeroed in on Australian rodeo and its western element. The favor He gave to us with everyone there was fantastic. It was obvious that most of those with whom we came in contact had heard little, if anything, about the Lord. Few of them had ever heard that Jesus Christ is the only way to heaven. I was especially touched to see Dennis leading an elderly man to the Lord after explaining to him the love of God in sending Jesus. The old man ecstatically shook Dennis' hand, thanking him and saying, "Just think. God sent a cowboy all the way from the United States just so I wouldn't have to go to hell."

Among those in attendance at our Australian services was a young bronc rider, Tim Kelly. Tim committed his life to Jesus during this time and demonstrated a real hunger for the things of God. Unknown to me at the time, God had Tim earmarked to play a part in conjunction with our ministry to reach the Australian western world.

When the World Cup Rodeo moved its activities to Sydney, we moved our services to the rodeo grounds there, meeting in the bleachers and in the hotel. God continued to pour out His Spirit, saving souls and meeting every type of need. Because many who had recently given their lives to the Lord needed and desired to be water baptized, we requested and received permission from the hotel to use their pool on the roof of the building. There, several of Australia's best in rodeo followed the Lord Jesus in scriptural water baptism. This scene was repeated several times in the next few years.

Although the World Cup Rodeo dissolved prematurely in corruption (underworld figures attempted to rip off the entire box office and funding), God had made His notch in Australian rodeo and would continue what He had begun. We returned home to the United States rejoicing in the effectiveness of God's sovereign move

Down Under and over the many precious brothers and sisters newly born into His kingdom. It was hard to leave, and until the moment of departure, it appeared that I was going to have to leave Dennis behind. He could hardly tear himself away from the new converts.

We made other junkets into Australia—yearly, for a while. Each time we witnessed God's Word permeating more deeply into the heart and core of both rodeo and western oriented folks. We fell in love with the beautiful country and its forthright people. We began to hold meetings not only at rodeos but also in a rented hall in Warwick, Queensland, where the Australian Rough Riders Association is headquartered. There, we had many cowboys and girls in attendance and lots of local people. God gloriously saved, healed, baptized, and met many other needs. Close friendships were formed. One young lady who became especially dear to our hearts is Jennie Shean, a former Miss Rodeo Australia. She desired to receive the baptism in the Holy Spirit, and when Ann prayed for her, she began to speak in flawless French. Jennie went out of her way to make our stay in her home town of Warwick comfortable.

Returning a few years after the World Cup Rodeo, Ann and I felt Willard Moody was to go with us. In order to go to the rodeos in some of the Outback areas, we leased through our local travel agency the best motor home that could be rented in Australia. It was the only one boasting an inside toilet; it proved to be a por-table toilet that sat in the shower. When we arrived in Brisbane, tired from our long journey, Andy Gay was there to meet us. Andy had attended the World Cup services, having been saved a short time before. A stable young man in the Lord, Andy desired to come to the United States. We had agreed that he would drive for us during our motor home travels in Australia; then we would take him home with us to the U.S. for a few months.

Andy was ready and rearing to go. We wanted to sleep for a while in our nice rooms at the hotel before heading to the rural areas. Willard went to the room he would share with Andy. Ann and I retired to ours.

Before we could go to sleep, our phone rang. It was Dennis. He had preceded us into Australia by several weeks. He would return to the United States shortly after we arrived. By overlapping our trips, we felt we could more effectively minister longer and to more people.

We could tell by Dennis' tone that he was concerned. He said many wonderful things had happened, with many receiving the Lord. However, he had run into a real problem at one of the rodeos up north and felt we should know about it as soon as possible. He didn't want us encountering difficulty in ignorance. It seems Dennis had been ministering at a rodeo and was preparing to preach in the grandstand on a Sunday morning. Suddenly a group of rodeo "toughs" appeared and stood by Dennis in front of the crowd. They were loud and unruly, saying and doing all sorts of things to prevent Dennis from preaching the gospel. He asked them several times in a nice way to step aside while he ministered the Word. (They were especially hostile to Dennis because Dennis had been winning the calf roping at most of the rodeos he attended. They didn't like his Christianity or his outstanding performance as a roper.)

The group's ringleader, a longtime rodeo professional, was resentful and hostile to God's entrance into rodeo. He determined to put an end to the services, as well as the American contestants invading his territory. He threatened to whip Dennis, then taunted him, saying, "But I know you Christians have to turn the other cheek if I hit you." That was enough for Dennis. He hadn't spent many years prior to his conversion literally fighting his way through life for nothing!

Dennis laid down his Bible, asking the crowd to excuse him for a moment. He spoke to the Australian tough, who had quite a fighting reputation. "Come over here with me and we'll settle this." Dennis walked a ways aside, still in view of the rodeo church crowd, who were watching from the grandstand. The amazed Australian cowboy followed him, startled that his bluff had been called. He still didn't believe that Dennis would hit him. He was banking on the "weakness" of Dennis' Christianity to prevent that. Again, he threatened Dennis, drawing back his fist to hit him. Dennis, a seasoned pre-Christ fighter, drew back and landed a blow that sent the Australian cowboy reeling. By the time the short-lived fight was over, the ringleader of the dissenters was flat on his back, assuring Dennis that he had had enough.

Dennis walked to his vehicle, put on a clean shirt, and returned to the grandstand, where an awed crowd awaited him. The troublemakers slunk away in embarrassment and shame as Dennis prepared to minister the Word of God. Telling the crowd, "I do not know whether or not what I did was right, but if I was wrong, I've asked God to forgive me, and He has." Proceeding with the service, Dennis preached, and souls were won to Jesus. It wasn't a typical Sunday morning church service, but God's purposes were not thwarted.

I was a little concerned when I heard Dennis's report. Willard, even though a very able fighter, having proved it in his heathen days, didn't need to begin his Australian ministry in this manner, and I certainly had no intention of engaging in physical combat with anyone. We began to pray, and within a short time the Lord had presented the following scripture to us: "When a man's ways please the LORD, he maketh even his enemies to be at peace with him" (Prov. 16:7). It was a huge relief to know that the Lord was intervening on our behalf.

All the time we ministered in Australia, He kept the group that had troubled Dennis at considerable length from us. We got wind of their threats and grumblings, but they could never touch us. In fact, God turned the enemy upon themselves. A man reported to be involved with the Australian underworld grabbed a hostile cowboy by the throat and announced that even though he was personally uninterested in the gospel, he intended to see to it that we were free to do what we had come to do, and he would personally attend to anyone who tried to prevent us. That definitely discouraged our opponents.

Another couple of fighting cowboys who were Christians, being newly born again but unconvinced that all fighting was evil, came to us saying, "You preach. We'll see to it that no one bothers you." And no one did.

Andy Gay, Ann, Willard, and I began our long, several-week journey throughout Australia in the little motor home we had leased. We soon discovered that the leasing company had put a governor on the motor home, preventing us from traveling at a speed of more than about eighty kilometers (about forty-five miles per hour). We were unenthusiastic about that, considering we had about thirty-six hundred miles to cover.

We traveled a good part of Australia holding services at rodeos. Although we were constantly interested in making new converts, it seemed this trip was primarily for the purpose of teaching the young believers and answering questions for the leaders God had raised up. The rodeo in Mt. Isa was a large one. Both Dennis and Willard placed in the calf roping before Dennis flew home.

Traveling the long, very narrow road to Alice Springs, I was convinced that we had exceeded God's command to "go ye into all the world." As I studied the red dirt, which was littered with huge termite mounds, I was amazed that the eucalyptus trees could survive. Considering the perfectly flat terrain, which stretched on seemingly endlessly, I thought of the beautiful rolling coastline of eastern Australia, some of it very tropical, and then of the small towns perched among green hills several miles inland. Truly, Australia, larger than the United States, has equally as diversified scenery.

Absolutely beautiful flocks of multicolored birds would often swarm into the sky. Herds of emus, tall birds resembling the ostrich, could occasionally be seen striding beside the fenceless road. Groups of kangaroo and wallaby frequented the landscape. How graceful they were! Unhappily, it was not uncommon, we found, to see many dead kangaroo and cattle lying beside the road. Rather than even consider fencing such a great expanse, cattlemen took their chances. When the Australian "road train" came barreling down the practically one-lane highway, everything got out of the way or got hit. (The road train resembles a large truck with several long trailers behind.) Multitudes of times we pulled our little motor home one wheel off the road to permit the flying road trains to pass. We observed that most Australian vehicles in the Outback sported "roo catchers"—curved screens on the front of the car or truck designed to scoop up kangaroos who chose to hop across the road in front of the vehicle, a common occurrence, especially at nighttime.

At Alice Springs and Tenant Creek (a town en route to Alice Springs) we were impressed with the large aboriginal population. A few of the gentle black original populace of Australia attended our meetings; we were thrilled to learn of the tremendous move of God taking place among their various tribes.

Impressed by the Holy Spirit to return to the coastal region instead of proceeding north to Darwin, as planned, I soon praised God that I had heard Him. Intending to return to Warwick in Queensland and hold a few meetings there before our trip home, we began the long trek back. Late one evening, the motor home gave up the ghost on the side of a hill near the little town of Gin-Gin. Ann and I waited while Willard and Andy hiked in to secure a wrecker, which towed us in to the tiny town. Renting a room with several beds in the more tolerable of the two motels we saw, it took our combined faith to make it through the night. I do not think the management had seen the necessity of changing sheets in the previous few years. We opted to sleep in our clothes and did not move one inch more than necessary. At midnight we burst into spontaneous laughter, which continued for quite a while. Some missionaries we were!

Relieved when the motor home leasing company sent a car for us, which we drove to Brisbane, we were soon in another motor home and on our way to Warwick. After holding a few meetings there and visiting with friends, we returned to Brisbane, then caught a flight to Sydney.

On a previous trip to Australia, we stayed briefly in a Sydney hotel. Ann and I were in the lobby getting ready to leave when Ann glanced over at the elevator and saw a lady, perhaps in her late forties. The Holy Spirit stirred within her heart, saying, "That lady is in dreadful need." Ann stood and walked toward the elevator, which was still open. It appeared that the lady was going right back into the elevator, and that is exactly what she did. The door reopened, and Ann stepped inside with the sad-looking woman.

"I don't know what is troubling you, but I want you to know that the Lord loves you. He cares about you and wants to help you."

Ann put her hand on the woman's shoulder. The

lady began to cry. "I came over here on a tour from the United States," she wept. "My husband just died, and I don't know what to do or where to go. I thought I could run away and find peace if I took a trip like this, but I am alone and miserable."

Ann began to share the love of Jesus with the heart-broken soul, who listened intently and gratefully. When the elevator returned once more to the lobby floor, they stepped outside and sat down while Ann outlined through the Scriptures the need to be born again. The lady eagerly received God's Word and gladly prayed to receive Jesus into her heart. In a few minutes after Ann had secured the woman's United States address for further follow-up, they parted joyfully with the lady exclaiming, "Isn't it amazing! I had to come all the way over here to find the Lord!"

It is interesting to note that Rev. Smith Wigglesworth is reported to have prophesied that when the Lord begins to move mightily in Australia, look out! The second return of Jesus is just around the corner. Without the shadow of a doubt, the Spirit of God is hovering over that nation.

Chapter Fifteen
MINISTRIES SPAWNED AND SCATTERED

FEELING THAT AUSTRALIA would be reached, for the larger part, by Australians, we began to pray for God's leadership in regard to establishing an office Down Under. It soon became apparent that He had, as I mentioned earlier, Tim Kelley selected for the headship of such an office. We knew that the Lord would have us commit substantial monthly sums to such an office. We would also do everything possible to supply literature and Bibles. Tim, a young man of integrity, was certain of the call of the Lord on his life. When asking the Lord about whether he should quit his job as a butcher ("at a meatworks," an Australian would say), the Lord caused the following scripture to leap off the page of Tim's Bible: "Labour not for the meat which perisheth, but for that meat which endureth unto everlasting life" (John 6:27). What more appropriate scripture could be spoken to a man who made his living working with physical meat every day? I assure you: God is able to instruct us through His Word.

Tim and his family continue to do a bang-up job for the Lord, reaching deep into the Australian western world, snatching lost souls from their destination of a fiery hell. Printing their version of our American ministry newsletter, *The Conqueror,* they use many of our articles but adapt the newsletter to an Australian format. As the Lord has lead, we continue to travel to Australia every so often.

Richard Ashley, the young Californian who came to us many years ago in Cheyenne, lived on our ministry premises for a couple of years, studying and learning the ropes so to speak. He placed himself in a servant's position, and God began to exalt him. Feeling led to go to Saltillo, Coahuila, Mexico, to learn Spanish, Richard did just that and found his niche in ministry by doing so. Richard began to minister the gospel to Mexican cowboys and girls and to involve himself in the Mexican version of rodeo. He also travels to various ranches and rural groups spreading the good news. Marrying a local Saltillo young lady, Susana, who is a strong and dedicated Christian, Richard is reaching Spanish-speaking people with God's love. At one rodeo school, all fifty participants stood up to receive Jesus when the invitation was given.

As for Ann and me personally, we have relinquished many of our rodeo services to other ministries. We continue to minister largely in ranching and rural areas, although many other doors are opening. Invitations from foreign countries continue to come. Ann and I both desire to follow Jesus and His plan for our lives and ministry whatever the cost. Both of us deeply desire to go into areas and to peoples where no one has blazed the trail. I believe our Father is honoring that desire and giving us more new territory—to His glory and praise.

Chapter Sixteen

HOW MUCH GOD LOVES YOU!

YOU ARE HIS special creation. It is His heart's desire that you give your life to Him, permitting Him to love, lead, and bless every area of your life as you obey and serve Him.

To become God's child, you just go through His Son, Jesus Christ. He alone is the way, the path to God the Father and to heaven. The Bible tells us, "I [Jesus] am the way, the truth, and the life: no man cometh unto the Father, but by me" (John 14:6).

God loves us so much that He sent His Son, Jesus, to earth to live the sinless life we could not live and then to die on a cross at Calvary in payment for our sins. He took our sins, shedding His blood to wash them away, so that we could be in right standing with God and live eternally with Him (2 Cor. 5:21).

The Bible says that all have sinned and have need of Him (Rom. 3:23). No matter how many wrong things you have done, you can receive forgiveness and a new life by simply receiving Jesus and accepting what He has done for you. John 1:12 promises, "But as many as received him, to them gave he power [the right or privilege] to become the sons of God, even to them that believe on his name."

Will you pray and invite Jesus into your heart,

trusting Him as your very own Savior and Lord? If so, sincerely pray the following prayer:

> *Lord Jesus, I receive You and all that You have done for me. I want to take the path to heaven, and I see that You are the only way. Forgive my sins. I commit my life to You. Thank You for giving me eternal life. Teach me to understand Your Word.*
>
> *Heavenly Father, thank You that I am Your child because of Jesus and His shed blood, in Jesus' name, amen.*

If you prayed that prayer, you are now a child of God and are assured of eternal life. Welcome to His family! Let us know of your decision to receive Jesus, and we will send you helpful literature to aid you in your new Christian walk.

If you will keep your eyes on Jesus, He will lead you victoriously through this earthly life and into the one to come. He who rode an unbroken colt into Jerusalem when He lived upon the earth will be riding a white horse when we see Him again (Rev. 19:11–14).

\- \- \- \- \- \- \- \- \-

For additional copies of this book, contact your local bookstore or visit our Web site at www.rodeocowboy ministries.org.

International Headquarters

International Western World Outreach Center
Aka Rodeo Cowboy Ministries
P O Box 1230
Midland, Texas, 79702-1230

Australian Office

Rodeo Cowboy Ministries
P O Box 905
Kingaroy, Queensland 4610

ABOUT THE AUTHOR

GLENN SMITH, FOUNDER and president of International Western World Outreach Center, Inc. (a.k.a. Rodeo Cowboy Ministries), was an ex-rodeo professional and rancher.

Ministering the gospel with a western flavor, Glenn was ordained to full-time ministry in the early nineteen seventies.

Preaching and teaching the uncompromised Word of God, Glenn and his wife, Ann, have traveled throughout the U.S. and many other countries. International Western World Outreach Center has established offices in Australia and Mexico, as well as the central office in the U.S.

With special emphasis on the western world, Glenn has pioneered many cowboy church services and camp-meetings, including those at the National Finals Rodeo and the World Cup Rodeo in Australia. As a result of the extreme move of God in the western world, an explosion of cowboy churches has occurred throughout this country as well as others.